"Ralph Muncaster speaks layman to layman about the scientific evidences for intelligent design. Most helpful is the wealth of historical material that helps make his discussion about the latest scientific discoveries both fun to read and understandable."

—HUGH ROSS, PHD, ASTROPHYSICIST, FOUNDER
OF REASONS TO BELIEVE INSTITUTE, AND AUTHOR
OF *THE CREATOR AND THE COSMOS*

"Dismantling Evolution raises many hard questions about the common point of view that we are a product of chance, from the origin of life to the evolution of the species. Those holding this view should objectively consider the facts in light of the recent scientific breakthroughs presented by Ralph Muncaster."

—ROGER C. WIENS, PHD, A SPACE PHYSICIST IN
CHARGE OF SPACECRAFT INSTRUMENTS AT LOS
ALAMOS NATIONAL LABORATORIES

"The dismantling of Darwinian evolution is long overdue, and Ralph Muncaster shows how intelligent design is dismantling this outdated dogma. This book will be particularly helpful to the general reader looking for an easily accessible introduction to intelligent design."

—DR. WILLIAM DEMBSKI, AUTHOR OF
*INTELLIGENT DESIGN: THE BRIDGE BETWEEN
SCIENCE AND THEOLOGY*

"Researcher Ralph Muncaster admirably communicates the latest and most compelling evidences for intelligent design from a wide range of scientific disciplines, explaining why it's only a matter of time before the scientific community at large will have no choice but to reject naturalism."

—DR. FAZALE RANA, BI<

D0150049

Dismantling EVOLUTION

Ralph O. Muncaster

HARVEST HOUSE™ PUBLISHERS

EUGENE, OREGON

Cover by Terry Dugan Design, Minneapolis, Minnesota

DISMANTLING EVOLUTION
Copyright © 2003 by Ralph O. Muncaster
Published by Harvest House Publishers
Eugene, Oregon 97402

Library of Congress Cataloging-in-Publication Data
Muncaster, Ralph O.
    Dismantling evolution / Ralph O. Muncaster.
        p. cm.
    Includes bibliographical references.
    ISBN 0-7369-0464-6 (pbk.)
    1. Evolution (Biology)   2. Creationism.   I. Title.
        QH367 .M86 2003
        231.7′652—dcc21   20002011818

Printed in the United States of America

03 04 05 06 07 08 09 10 11 / RDP-MS / 10 9 8 7 6 5 4 3 2 1

To the many esteemed scientists and mathematicians
to whom we owe our vast knowledge of the way things are,
especially those who probe into the far reaches of the cosmos,
those who peer into the depths of cells and cellular systems,
and those who perform mathematical probability analysis.

Without their fine work,
we could never fully recognize the impossibility
of neo-Darwinian evolution.

Without their fine work,
we could never fully appreciate the glory of God.

Contents

Things Aren't Always the Way They Appear 9

Part 1 — A Bridge Between Nonlife and Complex Life

1. Flaws in the Structure 19
2. Steps to Span the Gap 29

Part 2 — A Look at the Bridge's Components

3. Hard Evidence Versus Soft Evidence 45
4. Observation: Examining Things Logically 57
5. The Myths of Evolution 63
6. The Fossil Record 77

Part 3 — Another View of the Bridge

7. From Atoms to the First Cell 93
8. From the First Cell to 1.7 Million Species 103

Part 4 — The Micro: Dismantling the Old Span, Building a New One

9. The Complexity of Living Cells 117
10. Chirality: There's No Solution in Sight 131
11. The Probability of the Random Origin of the
    First Living Cell 137
12. Mutations: A Faulty Mechanism 147
13. Irreducible Complexity: A Major Transitional
    Problem 159
14. Nanotechnology: Engineers Copy Our Own
    Cellular Machines 173
15. Intelligent Design and Information Theory 183

Part 5 — The Macro: Moving from a Flawed Structure to a Firm One

16. Physics: How Do We Explain the Contradiction
    Between Two Natural Laws? 195

17. A Finely Tuned Universe: What Are the Odds? 209

    Summing Up: How to Build a Strong Bridge 217

    Appendix A: Some Evidences That a Planet Was
                Designed to Support Life 225

    Appendix B: How Old Are the Earth and the
                Universe? 231

    Appendix C: The Original Source of Evidence
                for a Beginner 239

    Notes 241

    Bibliography 252

Things Aren't Always the Way They Appear

What does a long bridge stretched over a deep canyon have in common with the idea of evolution? Both span a vast chasm, and both offer a possible means of getting from one side to the other. Both require a number of things to work right if a successful crossing is to be made.

The bridge offers a structure designed by engineers that presumably will withstand the weight it's intended to bear. Evolution relies on a body of interrelated evidence that is presumably strong enough to answer the question of how the first living cell came about and then developed into more than a million identified species.[1]

In the case of the bridge, everything from the beams to the bolts must be strong, or it will fall. Failure of one major component means disaster. In the case of evolution, the entire sequence of evidence must be strong, or the theory will fall apart. One broken element in the evolutionary span is all it takes for the theory to be false.

What I Was Taught

Most of my life I felt certain about naturalistic evolution.* Why shouldn't I be certain? After all, I'd been taught the concept of evolution—"molecules to man"—since the sixth grade.

I'd heard many of the details of evolution: that the first living cell developed in a rich primordial "soup" that provided the perfect chemistry for its formation. That over billions of years the first cells changed, through mutation, into more complex cells, which in turn mutated into multicelled creatures, which eventually mutated into many types of multicelled creatures. That, according to neo-Darwinian theory, these life forms continued to become more and more complex as mutant alternatives were sorted out by natural selection. That older species transitioned into newer ones that were better suited to survive. It all seemed to make sense. And there seemed to be plenty of evidence. I believed it.

First, there was evidence in the fossil record. I was told that some transitional species had been found in ancient bones. One of the examples that was often presented was the archaeopteryx, a reptile–bird that appeared in almost every textbook. Though this creature had feathers, it also had some features of a reptile—teeth, a tail, and claws on its wings. Several archaeopteryx fossils had been found. It seemed to be evidence of a transitional species.

Then there was the "tree of evolution," based primarily on the species classification developed by Carolus Linnaeus in the 1700s. This methodology places creatures into broad categories that are successively broken down into more specific categories—eventually, down into individual species, groups that can reproduce within themselves.

---

* Throughout this book I use the word "evolution" to refer to the theory (or group of theories) that attempts to explain the origin and development of life as occurring "naturalistically" through increasing complexity over time. Webster's dictionary defines *naturalism* as "The doctrine that scientific laws are adequate to account for all phenomena." In other words, everything that exists can be explained by what we can now see or otherwise observe.

  Further, I also am referring to the *neo-Darwinian* version of evolutionary theory, which combines Darwin's original propositions about natural selection with discoveries from modern genetics. The development of the neo-Darwinian theoretical synthesis started around the beginning of the 1900s.

I was taught that this classification tree, combined with the dating of fossils that had features similar to today's animals, was clear evidence of evolution. For example, it was said that animals with similar characteristics had a similar ancestor. (This area of evolutionary study is called *homology*.)

Likewise the study of embryos *(embryology)* showed that remnants of various evolutionary ancestors exist in the embryos of today's animals. Drawings in textbooks illustrated that the embryos of various creatures appeared almost identical. Human embryos were said to have gill slits, a remnant of a tail, and a yolk sac—all indicating that humans came from more primitive creatures that had tails (reptiles or other mammals), gills (fish), and eggs (reptiles or birds).

When I asked my teachers what caused all the species to advance up the evolutionary ladder, they told me that positive mutation caused it. They showed me pictures of fruit flies that had mutated from exposure to radiation. Although the flies displayed strange and obviously harmful mutations, we were told that once in a while a positive mutation occurred. Then, "natural selection" would allow only the strongest to survive. And eventually, all these changes would lead to an entirely new species. At the time it seemed very logical.

There even appeared to be hard evidence that humans were at the threshold of creating life. My textbooks discussed the Miller–Urey experiments, which had synthetically produced some of the basic building blocks of life. Miller and Urey had created some amino acids that were necessary for life in an environment said to replicate that of the early earth. To me, this was the "smoking gun" that proved that evolution was probably possible, given billions of years to put all the pieces in place.

One day I was challenged by an acquaintance who believed in creation to reevaluate my strong belief in evolution. He said that recent developments in modern science, though fully understood by only the "elite" of the scientific world, were exposing the flaws in evolutionary theory. His arguments included hard-science findings that had been verified in only the past few years: A beginning of the universe had been confirmed. The age of the universe had been confirmed. General relativity had been confirmed. New light had been shed on DNA, RNA, and the development of proteins, revealing vast complexity that seemed to demonstrate elements of design.

This man challenged me with facts from modern research—facts I had never heard before. He indicated that today's evidence for "intelligent design" was based on the hard sciences of physics, molecular biology, mathematics, and statistics.

All this caused me to pause in my convictions about naturalistic evolution. But I certainly wasn't going to consider abandoning them without researching things for myself. After all, I had learned long ago that things aren't always the way they appear.

Things Aren't Always the Way They Appear

I loved my major at the University of Colorado—Engineering Design and Economic Evaluation. It was a highly creative engineering major that combined aspects of mechanical, civil, industrial, and electronic engineering. We were constantly challenged to "push the envelope" in solving problems. I spent many nights at the computer center determining optimum gear ratios, designing industrial engineering applications, or designing spans for bridges.

Solving such design problems was a lot of fun. While in college I was a national winner of the Lincoln Foundation award for the engineering design of a new product—a testing mechanism for ski bindings under a loaded condition. Later, I was called to testify in lawsuits as an engineering design expert. One lawsuit was against a prominent ski area. (I was hired as an expert because of my research in ski-binding testing.) Determining what made structures work or fail was always fascinating to me. It was like solving a mystery.

It was during my college training that I soon learned that things are not always the way they appear. For instance, look at the following diagrams and suggest which beam is stronger.

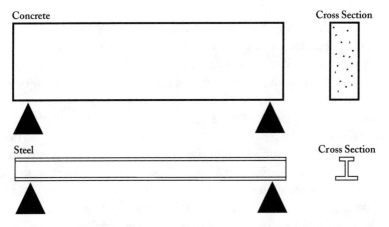

Many people would guess that the concrete beam is stronger because it is much larger, heavier, and more massive than the slender steel beam. Also, most people are aware of the enormous weight that concrete columns can support when loads are placed on top of them. Before the discoveries of modern engineering, it was believed that adding mass would add strength—even with beams.

But the appearance is deceiving. Concrete happens to be extremely strong in *compression* but relatively weak in *tension*. When a beam is loaded with weight, the top is under compression while the bottom is under tension. Steel, on the other hand, is extremely strong in both tension and compression.

Notice the "I-shape" of the steel beam. The majority of stress, especially on the tension side of the beam (the bottom) is compensated for with extra width, which gives extra strength. The same is true on the compression side.

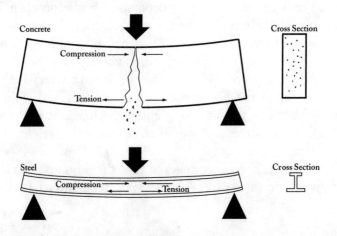

The diagram at the bottom of the previous page illustrates what would happen to a massive concrete beam without reinforcement on the bottom—the tension side. We see that the concrete fails under the load because of its weakness under tension. The I-beam compensates for the tension stress both by using a stronger material (steel) and by placing more steel on the tension and compression sides—where the maximum stresses occur. The connecting portion between the tension and compression sides needs to absorb only the lesser *shear* stresses within the beam. So when concrete is used for short spans, such as overpasses on freeways, it is *always* reinforced on the bottom with steel (this is called *prestressed* concrete). Well-designed house foundations also have steel re-bar near the bottom before concrete is poured. Once the concrete hardens, the foundation can then absorb the weight of a house and its contents.

So the thin, far lighter steel beam is much stronger than the unreinforced concrete beam. Sometimes, in fact, an unreinforced concrete beam can't even support its own weight. A relatively thin steel I-beam, on the other hand, will support not only its own weight, but much more. (The diagrams above picture a simple beam-type bridge that would be used for only very short spans. More complex structures are necessary when a bridge is being designed for longer spans.)

The Bridge of Evolution

When I was challenged about my strongly held belief in evolution, I realized I was facing a version of the bridge problem. I was being asked to believe that, first, a tiny bacterium had come from nonliving matter, and then that it had evolved into more than 1.7 million highly complex species. I immediately saw that the evidence supporting evolution would have to span a very large gap between nonlife and highly specialized human life. Was the evidence I had been taught strong enough? Or was it just a lot of unreinforced concrete that would crack under the weight of critical review?

No doubt my teachers believed that the amount of evidence supporting the theory of evolution was great. In fact I was told that the evidence was so massive that any "intellectual" person would be a fool not to accept it. Naturally I didn't want to be considered a fool, so for much of my life, I just accepted the theory as fact. Evolution, I was taught, was "scientific." Design by a Creator seemed simply supernatural. It seemed like only a hope with no facts to back it up. I was told that "creationists" were ignorant, prejudiced, and simply uninformed.

But now I had been challenged. I started to reflect upon the various bridge designs I'd studied, and how things aren't always the way they appear. Was evolution one such example? Could the bridge of evolution bear the weight of the latest findings?

I was determined to use the evidence of modern science, particularly in the areas of astrophysics and biochemistry—the "hot" new areas of burgeoning discoveries—to see if it could support evolution, or if something supernatural was necessary to explain life. I thought it would be easy to show that evolution was obvious, and that any idea of "intelligent design" by a "Creator" was absurd.

Certainly all my past teachers couldn't be wrong. Evolution had to be the basis for all life.

Part 1

A Bridge Between Nonlife and Complex Life

One

Flaws in the Structure

Evolution is described as a chain of events. Events as seemingly elementary as the origin of the first bacterium, which then evolved into the most complex creature now in existence—humans. However, I realized that a huge component of the bridge of evidence would be a mechanism capable of causing change. I also assumed that a long time would be necessary. I had been taught that the combination of mutations and billions of years could allow this to happen. I had assumed that those scientists who researched this theory for a living had "done their homework" and were correct. But I decided to do my own investigation anyway.

Reading Charles Darwin's book *On the Origin of the Species* seemed to be a good start. I was startled when I found out that Darwin had pointed out possible problems with his theory, problems that science is still struggling with today. For instance, in the introduction to a 1971 edition of *On the Origin of the Species* British biologist L. Harrison Matthews notes,

> The fact of evolution is the backbone of biology, and
> biology is thus in the peculiar position of being a sci-
> ence founded on an unproved theory—is it then a sci-
> ence or a faith? Belief in the theory of evolution is thus
> exactly parallel to belief in special creation—both are
> concepts which believers know to be true but neither,
> up to the present, has been capable to prove.[1]

This gave me warning that I might find potential flaws in the
bridge of evolution. As I continued my research, I found not just
one weak beam, or a problem with one section of the theory—I
found damaged parts throughout. In fact, I couldn't identify a
single section that was strong. All I turned up were a lot of "soft"
theories about how things "might have happened." There seemed
to be no solid empirical basis for these ideas.

Yet I fought the new information, still wanting to believe in
everything I'd been taught. I wanted to believe I was right and was
too bright to be fooled. For so many years I had been grounded in
the facts of evolution. Perhaps I was afraid to admit that new evidence actually favored a theory of design by some intelligent being.
Perhaps I had a deep-seated fear of accountability to a "designer"
who was greater than I was. I preferred that evolution be true.
Then, as simply a product of randomness, I would be ultimately
accountable to no one.

First Steps

I realized that a single major flaw in the evidence for the bridge
of evolution would destroy the theory, but I wanted to be absolutely
certain of the evidence before I talked to others—and perhaps even
faced being embarrassed in front of my engineering friends. So I
proceeded in my investigation with great care. Although I evaluated the "soft" evidence that had been presented to me so often
before, I was more interested in analyzing the new hard evidence
from astrophysics and molecular biology. (I explain more about
"hard" and "soft" evidence in chapter 6.)

Ultimately, I knew I would be faced with a decision. Could
the bridge of evolution be strengthened by the facts from new

discoveries? Could these new facts reinforce a bridge of evidence leading from nonliving matter to our world full of life? Or was the whole span patched together with anchors, beams, and connectors that looked strong, but in reality were weak?

Likewise, as I looked at the evidence I would evaluate whether a theory of "intelligent design" demonstrated a higher probability of explaining life's origin than naturalistic evolution.

I started reading some of the latest books by evolutionists to see how the theory had progressed in the last few years. As a believer in evolution, I was disturbed by my discovery that other evolutionists hedged their opinions, seeming to acknowledge faults in evolutionary theory. One noted evolutionist—John Maynard Smith, Emeritus Professor of Biology at the University of Sussex in Great Britain, along with his colleague Eors Szathmary of the Institute for Advanced Study in Budapest—stated,

> The theory of evolution by natural selection does not predict that organisms will get more complex. It predicts only that they will get better at surviving and reproducing in the current environment, or at least that they will not get worse.[2]

This statement amazed me. It acknowledges that, though changes can occur *within* a species through natural selection, more complex changes that cause one species to be transformed *into another* (that add complexity) are theoretically unfounded. It seemed as though evolution couldn't do what it was supposed to do.

Information Today Is Not Like It Was in the '60s and '70s

I was first introduced to evolution in the 1960s. With the advent of the computer age, however, new information started pouring in on us like never before. Many new tools became available, including supercomputers, space probes, and earth satellites.

Biochemistry experienced breakthroughs. Suddenly we were able both to chart the edges of the universe and also to peer into the depths of molecules. Now we have mapped the human DNA molecule, and molecular biology has given us insight into the living cell that we've never had before. Developments in engineering, astrophysics, and cosmology have allowed us to see the heavens with startling clarity. And supercomputers now enable us to mathematically and statistically evaluate and draw hard conclusions from the vast amounts of data we are now receiving.

The more I investigated all this new evidence about the origin of life and the development of the enormous number of complex species, the more I began to question the neo-Darwinian evolution I had been taught. In fact, the evidence was now pointing to intelligent design as the origin of the species. From the cosmos to the intricate depths of human cells, mathematical probability seemed to be supporting design over random origins through evolution.

Darwin's Problems

I was surprised when I discovered that the standard theory of evolution would today be opposed by its originator, Charles Darwin, based on his own writings. In his book *On the Origin of the Species*, Darwin wrote,

> Natural selection can act only by the preservation and accumulation of *infinitesimally small inherited modifications,* each profitable to the preserved being.[3]

However, recently many evolutionists have concluded that vast numbers of changes have occurred all at once at various points in history. Unfortunately for them, this both contradicts Darwin's statement and also points to intelligent design. The main piece of scientific evidence for this theory is the *Cambrian explosion* (so termed because it happened during the time scientists have named the Cambrian period).

The evidence from this period shows vast quantities of creatures experiencing substantial *non-infinitesimal* change—all within a relatively short time. In fact, gradualism is not supported anywhere in the fossil record. The term for this new theory that attempts to account for this is *punctuated equilibrium* (see chapter 6). This essentially means that evolution took place in very rapid spurts—at those times when new species were formed.*

Certainly this does not fit the neo-Darwinian model—and to me it seemed illogical. If the changes were significant enough to create entire new organisms, they certainly were not "infinitesimal," as Darwin concluded they had to be. Rather, this phenomenon seemed similar to the design of objects by human beings. For example, once we discovered the transistor, many uses for it were found, in all kinds of inventions (radios, computers, and so on)—all within a relatively short period of time. But "creators"—human engineers—intelligently designed these items. They did not come about through gradual, random changes.

Darwin was rightly disturbed by the lack of "transitional" species in the fossil record. He asked this question:

> But, as by this theory innumerable transitional forms must have existed, why do we not find them embedded in countless numbers in the crust of the earth?[4]

The existence of "transitional" species would imply that a creature was in a state of development between two species. For example, it might be a reptile with a partially formed feather, not a wholly developed one; or a creature with a part of an eye that didn't yet "work." Now, even though millions of fossils have been found since Darwin's time, we still can't identify any transitional species—let alone "countless numbers." In fact, in the fossil record body parts and systems are either fully formed or non existent. (More on this in chapter 7.)

Should We Criticize Darwin?

In a sense Darwin has been wrongly criticized. *He predicted problems in his theory that are still problems today.* And now new,

---

* Even though some theorists still hold to the viewpoint of punctuated equilibrium (which was more in favor in the late twentieth century), the body of evolutionists as a whole now favors the classical gradualistic form of evolution (see pages 86–87).

hard-science evidence is only adding to these difficulties. Darwin did well with the information he had at the time, but he developed his theory at the time of the American Civil War. What is harder to understand is why this 150-year-old theory (though somewhat modified) is still being taught as fact in light of recent discoveries.

Actually, when we look at Darwin's theory, we should remember his contribution of the idea of natural selection. Yes—natural selection seems to be valid in the "micro" sense—causing change *within* a species' existing DNA. We can even selectively breed plants and animals within their existing DNA structures. However, change *between* species has never been substantiated.

New Explanations?

Now, having much recent evidence that was unavailable to Darwin, how do modern evolutionists support their theory? It seems that, often, either they attempt to hold onto outdated ideas by the simple assumption that evolution is fact—or else the evidence is just ignored. In other cases they attempt to explain the theory's many problems by reaching into outer space for answers. For example, there is speculation that the "building blocks of life," such as amino acids, were "optically purified" (see chapter 9) in black holes, or by polarized light in outer space. Then they were swept to earth while being combined with hundreds of thousands of other "just right" compounds. And all this is said to have occurred at precisely the right point in time. All such theories are fraught with problems, however. (Chapters 10 and 11 explain more about this.)

Such new thinking is apparent in this comment by Maynard Smith and Szathmary:

> The problem of the origin of life is the problem of how entities with multiplication, variation, and heredity could arise, the starting-point being the chemical environment of the primitive Earth...But first, we must say a word about *the possibility that life originated elsewhere in the Universe, either accidentally or by deliberate action of extraterrestrials.*[5]

Are evolutionary theorists now so frustrated that they look to extraterrestrials as possible solutions to problems about the origin of life that can't be resolved? Moreover, this just puts the difficulties one step further away. It doesn't answer the question, "How did the extraterrestrials come to be?"

Did Evolutionists Do Their Math Homework?

When evolution was reaching one of its peaks of public exposure after the 1925 "Scopes Monkey Trial," most scientists thought the universe was infinite, both in duration and size. Now, thanks to the work of Einstein and others, we know that there was a beginning (see chapters 16 and 17). Thanks to space probes and high-powered telescopes, we can gauge the age of the universe—about 15 billion years. Now, thanks to breakthroughs in biochemistry, we have mapped the 3.2 billion base pairs of precisely oriented, precisely placed components of human DNA. (A *base pair* is like the rung of a ladder in the DNA structure—see chapters 9 and 10.)

These discoveries created a number of problems that I needed to consider mathematically. Was there enough *time* for the first cell to originate through naturalistic causes? Was there enough *time* to go from a single-celled creature, with perhaps as few as 100,000 base pairs of DNA, to complex creatures like humans, with 3.2 billion base pairs? If natural selection couldn't bring about greater complexity, then what was the *mechanism* for change? Where did the *information* come from to "tell" the DNA what to do? What about the statistical problem of the correct *molecular orientation* of amino acids and DNA—the chirality issue? (See chapter 10.)

I started to wonder why evolutionist writings consistently avoided the mathematics of evolution. Were they basing their theories simply on observational guesses, or was there hard evidence with statistics to back them up? Dr. Lee Spetner, who wrote an in-depth book on the mathematical probability of neo-Darwinian theories, pointed out a typical assumption of such writings. Referring to *The Blind Watchmaker*, a well-known book by evolutionist Richard Dawkins, Spetner commented,

Dawkins talked about chance, but he didn't calculate the chance of anything. Nor did he cite anyone who did. He just assumed that cumulative selection could lead to macroevolution. *He assumed what I have shown to be impossible.* He said, without justification: "Each successive change in the gradual evolutionary process was simple enough, relative to its predecessor, to have arisen by chance."[6]

Spetner's sentiment is echoed by astronomer Sir Frederick Hoyle. Regarding the origin of the first cell, Hoyle mathematically analyzed only one small portion of the chirality problem and concluded,

The likelihood of the formation of life from inanimate matter is one to a number with 40 thousand naughts [zeros] after it. It is enough to bury Darwin and the whole theory of evolution. There was no primeval soup, neither on this planet nor on any other, and if the beginnings of life were not random they must therefore have been the product of purposeful intelligence.[7]

Presupposition Precludes Objectivity

Even after encountering hard analyses like Spetner's and Hoyle's, it was difficult for me to start objectively questioning evolution and considering intelligent design. After all, I had always lived with the presupposition that evolution was fact. Therefore, I began with a bias similar to that expressed by evolutionist Richard Goldschmidt. In the 1950s, this University of California professor declared,

Evolution of the animal and plant world is considered by all those entitled to judgment to be a fact for which no further proof is needed.[8]

This statement reflects the attitude of the time—an attitude that still pervades the educational system today. Is it any wonder I just accepted naturalistic evolution as fact? Ironically, Goldschmidt also clearly understood that no proof existed for any interspecies change through "macromutation":

> It is true that nobody thus far has produced a new species or genus, etc., by macromutation. It is equally true that nobody has produced even a species by the selection of micromutations.[9]

As I read the self-contradictions of evolutionary scientists, my doubts increased. If there was no hard evidence to support the naturalistic evolutionary claim, then presupposing it as fact was certainly unscientific. After all, engineers would never propose building a bridge without hard measurements and observations. They would insist on having facts that had been tested by the scientific method—tested enough so that results could be predicted. Otherwise, lives would certainly be lost. Think of how much we owe to such hard science: The cars we drive, the planes we fly in, the buildings we work in are all based on its principles. But I discovered that evolution is not. Rather, it is based on presuppositions arising from simple observation and conjecture.

Is It Time for the New to Replace the Old?

As I studied the question of the origin of the species, I was determined that my research would not begin from the presuppositions of evolution I had been taught in school. Starting from this new viewpoint, I soon realized that the theory is stuck in its own old evidence. With new evidence mounting, I saw that some evolutionists are wondering what direction to take. Stephen Jay Gould noted,

> I think I can see what is breaking down in evolutionary theory—the strict construction of the modern synthesis with its belief in pervasive adaptation, gradualism, and extrapolation by smooth continuity from causes of change in local populations to major trends and transitions in the history of life. [This is the entire basis of

neo-Darwinism.] I do not know what will take its place
as a unified theory.[10]

After recognizing flaws in the bridge of evolutionary evidence,
I began to slowly—and reluctantly–change my mind. But I went
a step further than Gould. I addressed the likelihood of intelligent
design.

What I began to find excited me. It seemed that there *was*
something to take the place of evolutionary theory. I discovered
that living organisms are more like machines than people realize.
I even found that the latest microbiology is now *trying to duplicate*
biological "machines," which appear to be designed (see chapter
14). Molecular biologists hope that the study of these intricate,
effective, and efficient cell-based machines may lead to some of
the most amazing engineering breakthroughs ever known.[11]

Which Bridge?

I had a long way to travel from my reliance on evolutionary
theory. But the more I studied the facts, the more obvious it
became that someone had *designed* everything—from the carefully
constructed heavens that are so perfect for life, down to the intricate details of cell structure. Dr. Lee Spetner, who holds a PhD in
physics from MIT and accepted a fellowship in their department
of biophysics, expressed my findings in a nutshell:

> Random variations cannot lead to the large-scale evo-
> lution claimed by the neo-Darwinians…There is a lot
> of evidence for nonrandom [purposeful, therefore intel-
> ligent] variation.[12]

After studying the evidence that I present in this book, I came
to see that the interpretation that points to an intelligent designer
is actually far more "scientific" than the evolutionary interpretation. It is 1) more objective, 2) based on more hard evidence, and
is thus 3) more compelling.

Which kind of bridge would you rather cross?

Two

Steps to Span the Gap

Ashley lay motionless on the hospital bed. Even now, her eyes still reflected a faint sparkle of the liveliness of a six-year-old with all of life ahead of her. But this was not her typical day of carefree playing with the other kids in the neighborhood. No…her afternoon had not ended as usual—going over to her best friend Melinda's house for a snack.

Crowded around the bed were Ashley's mother, father, brother Michael, and her friend Melinda. A sense of sorrow and grief hung in the air. The images from the afternoon kept cutting through her mother's mind like a knife. The ball…the laughter of the children…the street…Ashley laughing…Then the screech of tires—laughter turned to screams—and her little girl lay face down on the asphalt, unmoving.

Now she was barely hanging onto life. Ashley, a girl with enough energy to light up the entire neighborhood, just lay there with machines connected to her body. For now, the monotonous tone of the heart monitor reassured everyone that she was still clinging to life. Though Ashley was in critical condition, the doctors were allowing her family to visit in an attempt to boost her spirits.

Beep...beep...beep...beep...the heart monitor continued its reassuring pulse. Ashley's mother leaned down to give her a soft kiss. Her father whispered to her that he loved her. Her brother held her hand. Beep...beep...beep...*tone*—!

Her mother screamed out, "Her heart's stopped! Nurse, quick, get the doctor!" Her father jumped up and raced down the hall, looking for the first available doctor. The nurse's station announced over the loudspeaker, "Any available doctor needed in Room 201, stat! Any available doctor needed in Room 201, stat!"

Ashley's arms went limp. Her face started turning pale.

Though it seemed like an eternity, within a few moments two doctors were by her side. One moved the family away. The other started CPR. A tech quickly wheeled a heart defibrillator around the corner. Tears streamed down her mother's face as she frantically cried, "She's dead. Oh, dear God, help her. She's dead." Meanwhile the staff moved about in "organized chaos." One doctor was rushing to set up the machine. The tech was preparing Ashley for the application of the electrodes. A nurse was checking IVs and tubes. They all moved about purposefully as the family stood gazing in a stunned silence that was broken only by the sobs of Ashley's mother.

The paddles of the defibrillator were placed on Ashley's chest and an electric shock was applied. Her limp body seemed to jump a foot off the bed. *Tone*—the heart monitor continued its ominous sound. Another shock. *Tone*—no response. Another *tone*—and another. Then—beep...beep...beep...beep...the sound from the monitor was like a symphony to the family. Ashley's mother started to rush to her daughter's side but was held back by her father. It appeared that Ashley had cheated death, at least for now.

How Is Life Joined to Physical Compounds?

Every source of information about evolution or intelligent design—books, films, media presentations, and so on—tends to minimize the most important issue that needs to be addressed:

The critical question is—
how do inanimate molecules come to life in the first place?

Think about the first book or article you ever read on the evolution–design issue. What did it focus on? Fossils? Mutations? The artificial development of amino acids? The "anthropic principle"? Gene sequencing? The Cambrian explosion? Do books or articles ever deal with the most basic question of all—that of the infusion of life into chemical compounds?

Why do researchers and authors spend so little time discussing how life was generated in chemicals? In all likelihood, it's because that is the topic researchers know the least about. It's also a topic that, almost by definition, requires speculation—be it from evolutionists or creationists. For someone who accepts intelligent design, such speculation is straightforward—a supernatural being (such as God) generated life supernaturally. For the evolutionist, who insists upon naturalistic explanations, the question is unanswerable. Further, the consideration of God is often repulsive. However, cutting through all other aspects of the study of origins, the infusion of life remains, by far, the most fundamental question of all.

Life itself is an extraordinary mystery. Consider Ashley. A vibrant six-year-old, full of life, was struck by a speeding vehicle. Suddenly, she was in critical condition, hanging onto "life" by a thread. Then for a few heart-wrenching minutes, her life seemed to have slipped away. Was Ashley really dead? Or, as the doctors were scrambling to "restart" her heart, was her brain still working, waiting for her heart to start pumping and delivering oxygen again? This issue, raised by the ability of modern medicine to "bring people back to life," has caused the medical profession to change the definition of death from "the cessation of heartbeat" to "the cessation of brainwaves." And now, even that is being called into question. So what is death, really? And what is life, really?

Most evolutionists would argue that life is a combination of chemical and electrical impulses acting on the physical parts of an organism to produce the actions associated with life. Webster defines it this way:

> The property or quality distinguishing living organisms
> from dead organisms and inanimate matter, manifested
> in functions such as growth, metabolism, response to
> stimuli, and reproduction.

This begs the question. Is life something natural? Or is it something supernatural? If it is natural, we would expect that evolution could create life. We might then ask, why can't we bring something back to life immediately after it dies by repairing the problem? Why doesn't this "inject" life back into it? After all, all the atoms and molecules are still essentially in the right place.

How about Ashley's case? It's not evidence of doctors "infusing" life into her dead body, because the body can survive for a period of time while deprived of oxygen. Restarting the heart quickly will provide that oxygen. But if Ashley's brain had failed as an organ, there would have been no known method of putting life back into her body.

Where Does Life "Live"?

There is another major problem evolutionists must answer if they deem the essence of life merely "natural." Everyone recognizes that the human body is made up of chemicals commonly found in dirt. But dirt can't perform the functions of a human being. Chemicals alone can't perform the functions of any living organism—without something else. So where does life "live"?

To further complicate the question, it is an accepted scientific fact that a human body has a total change of atoms about every five years. Author Richard Swenson, who is a medical doctor, notes in his book *More Than Meets the Eye,*

> According to isotope studies, 90 percent of our atoms
> are replaced annually. Every five years, 100 percent of
> our atoms turn over and become new atoms...
>   In the last hour, one trillion trillion of your atoms
> have been replaced.[1]

Others express this process in different terms. David M. Baughan, MD, says,

> We are continually being recreated from dust and returning to dust…We are not objects or machines that endure, we are patterns that have the capacity to perpetuate ourselves. We are not things; instead we are processes.[2]

Physicist John Tyndall states,

> Life is a wave, which in no two consecutive moments of its existence is composed of the same particles.[3]

So if the material of our body is constantly "turning over," with a total changeover every five years, how can we account for a person's staying the same? How do all the new cells have a memory of the past? How is the personality of an individual maintained? How are emotions transferred to new cells? Naturalistic evolution—indeed, any materialistic philosophy—has no answers to these most basic questions about life itself.

Life is clearly something more than just chemicals—chemicals that can be dug out of the ground. We can't measure it, we can't experience it directly, and we certainly can't manufacture or create it. At best, we can only move it from one already living thing to another.

So this book will share the flaw of all the others. It will focus on what we can understand—things like molecular biology, physics, and statistics. But I want to point out that, even if evolution had answers to the problems in these areas, the overriding question of *life itself* would still be far from being solved. With that in mind, let's proceed to the basic steps that must happen for evolution to bridge the gap between nonlife and the complex life we see on earth today.

THE BASIC STEPS IN THE SEQUENCE

Evolutionary theory contends that the appropriate atoms somehow came together to form life, and that this life eventually became transformed into the most complex "machines" known to us: human beings. Like a complex bridge, this process had to span a vast chasm by means of literally trillions of changes. The changes required certain key transitions in order to progress. If a single transition failed to happen, the entire bridge of evolution would collapse.

In building an effective bridge, the essential problem is putting together a vast array of components in the right order. If we were to break the bridge of evolution down into its five most basic sequential components, they would be as follows:

1. The bringing together of the basic structural parts for the first cell

2. The infusion of life into the first cell

The diversification of the first cell into today's highly complex species

3. The development of *asexually* reproducing single-celled organisms into *sexually* reproducing single-celled organisms

4. The development of *single-celled* organisms into *multicelled* organisms

5. The development of *multicelled* organisms into more than 1.7 million species

This simplification should not diminish the fact that, if evolution is to work, in reality there would have to be countless trillions of steps. Individual atoms would have to change within DNA, thus creating billions of individual changes leading to more than a million species. Also, we must keep in mind that a broken component anywhere causes the entire bridge of evolution to fail.

Step 1: The Right Stuff at the Right Place at the Right Time

All of us know that the universe is big—*very* big. So we all have the impression that there is a lot of "stuff" out there from which things could randomly come together. If we were to break the universe down into atoms, and from there into subatomic particles, this would yield a lot of matter from which to put together the first living cell. Now logically, we should limit ourselves to planet earth because this is the only place where we know that life exists. That would still give us a lot of matter to work with. But to be very generous with our estimates, let's take into account *all the matter in the entire universe* and *the entire time that the universe*—not just earth—*has existed.*

Scientists agree that there are about 10^{84} subatomic "pieces" (baryons) that make up the entire universe. The age of the universe is also estimated to be about 15 billion years. (Again, we're being generous, because the earth itself is estimated to have been around for only about 4.6 billion years.) Though some think that the universe is much younger (see appendix B), for our purposes we'll take the longer scientific estimates.

Fifteen billion years seems like a *lot* of time. But within this period of time, can we reasonably expect to have all of the specific atoms in the right sequence at precisely the right place at precisely the same time in order to provide the necessary requirements for life?

Evolutionary theorists say the very first organism would have been a single bacterium or blue-green algae cell, or a similar *prokaryotic* cell (a cell without a nucleus). However, there are far more atoms and far more specificity required for the construction of the simplest cell than we might think. One example of the complexity necessary is that all amino acids (in proteins) and nucleotides (in DNA) must have the correct molecular orientation. This issue of *chirality* alone, in just these cellular components, raises an enormous mathematical problem. But beyond chirality, there is still the problem of obtaining the correct sequencing of atoms—and the correct atoms to begin with—to form proper DNA, RNA, and protein chains. We then have to determine whether they could all arrive at the same place on earth (or elsewhere in the universe) at the same time. (These issues are examined in chapters 9 and 10.)

Finally, we have to determine if there is enough time for this to happen randomly (naturalistically). At least on the surface, it might seem quite feasible to get life started within a period of 15 billion years. But when we weigh the hard evidence, we must mathematically evaluate all the factors required. Viewed this way, evolutionary theories of the origin of life face a far greater challenge than would be expected.

Step 2: Putting Life into the First Cell

Once all the "stuff" is at the right place at the right time, then something must occur to add life. Assuming that all the components have properly bonded in a way that would support life, something needs to then *trigger it*—like the winding of a watch. All of the materials of a watch might be in the right place at the right time, but until it's wound, it's useless. Perhaps life could have started with an electrical discharge. Perhaps it could have started some other way. But this is the second major step in the evolutionary bridge.

Some contend that life started at a place other than planet earth. Beyond the fact that this scenario is unlikely, the steps still remain the same. Life still had to be somehow "injected" into "stuff" that was somehow put together properly. Furthermore, whatever transport mechanism would have brought that life to planet earth (the only known place in the universe that supports life) would have had to enable it to survive the trip. (In spite of complete lack of evidence, it has been suggested that aliens brought the first life forms to earth. But even if that were the case, we would still be faced with determining what started the aliens' evolution.) However, when we mathematically examine the origin of the first form of life, we will assume that it could have started anywhere in the universe and could have somehow been transported to the earth. We want to make sure that all possible scenarios are considered.

Step 3: Asexually Reproducing Life Forms Change into Sexually Reproducing Ones

This is a bigger step than most people might realize. To understand this, let's consider the difference between a cell that produces *asexually* and one that produces *sexually*.

Most evolutionary theorists suggest that the first cell was *prokaryotic* (a cell without a distinct nucleus)—probably a bacterium or blue-green algae cell. Such cells reproduce by *binary fission*. In other words, they simply split in two, and the two halves then each grow into a complete cell. This process is *asexual*.*

Most of the more complex *eukaryotic* cells (cells with a distinct nucleus), which we find in humans and many other life forms, reproduce themselves through a much more involved process called *mitosis*. It starts with a four-stage sequence in which the cell's nucleus reproduces itself. The mitosis is then completed by the division of the entire cell in two, each half containing one of the new nuclei.

Meiosis (*sexual* reproduction) adds yet another layer of complexity. Through this process, which is much more involved than mitosis, individual cells can exchange DNA by producing male and female *gametes*. (In humans the gametes are, respectively, sperm and eggs.) Each gamete contains half of the necessary DNA for a complete cell. When it joins with a gamete of the opposite sex, it forms a complete new cell that, even though it comes from the parent cells, does not completely match either of them.

According to evolutionary theory, eukaryotic cells represent the beginning of the chain of more complex creatures. Why? Because they allow more freedom of mutation through the exchange of DNA between cells (or entire organisms). In contrast, the simpler binary fission found in prokaryotic cells results in an exact replica of the original cell's DNA. Although a prokaryotic cell's DNA can mutate by some exterior means (like exposure to ultraviolet light)

---

* Even so, prokaryotic cells have an occasional resemblance of being sexual, since some replications of DNA allow for input of changed information—for example, through conjunction.

or by transcription, evolution needs some mechanism to bring about a substantial structural DNA change from one species to the next.

But where did the input of information come from to cause these huge changes? What "organized" and diversified the components of that first prokaryotic bacterium so that it changed into a eukaryotic cell, which has a nucleus and a sexual reproduction system? The gap that needs to be spanned to account for this new mechanism is much vaster than we might think. (For one thing, evlutionists say, there is an apparent span of time between the first prokaryotic cells and "evolved" eukaryotic cells of some 2 billion years.)

A couple of suggestions have been made. Perhaps there may have been a *second* organism that "assisted" in the mutational process. A virus may have been coincidentally formed at the same time at the same place, and it infected the simple bacterium and increased its complexity. Or perhaps a second bacterium with different traits was formed at the same place and time and interacted with the first cell through *conjunction*, or direct transfer of DNA. This then allowed for mutations that increased complexity.

However, when we consider the size of a simple bacterium (about 1/50,000 of an inch), getting two such randomly developed organisms at the same place at the same time seems enormously improbable. Thus, if evolutionists theorize that life began with the simplest life form (one reproducing by binary fission), this may actually complicate the problem of the start of life.

The alternative is that the first cell was actually a far more complex bacterium—with more DNA base pairs, cell "organs" *(organelles),* and a nucleus. In other words, it was a eukaryotic cell. However, this vastly complicates the problem of getting all the right elements together at the right place at the right time to form it in the first place. (For instance, studies by molecular biologists indicate that even the *cytoskeleton*—the complex membrane of eukaryotic cells—was necessary to properly orient proteins in the first living eukaryotic cell.)[4] Either way, the statistical odds must be considered, which I do in chapter 11.

Step 4: Individual Cells Develop into Multicelled Organisms with Specialized Organs

Consider a single cell. To provide an idea of size, about 1000 "typical" cells would fit into the period at the end of this sentence. This step of evolution would require that a single-celled organism somehow develop into something that not only has multiple cells, but eventually develops specialized cells and organs. Cells in a typical mammal's body include hair cells, blood cells, bone cells, nerve cells, and skin cells, to mention just a few.

Radical restructuring of the DNA in individual cells would have to occur for this step to be achieved. In fact, the DNA instructions would have to go far beyond simply enabling the cell to reproduce itself. They would have to enable precise sorting and "planning" of necessary organs and functions in the more complex organism. So one key question is, as before, from where does the organizing and developmental information come?

Step 5: The Development of Multicelled Organisms into More than 1.7 Million Species, Including Humans

This is the step that most people focus on. Maybe because it's where natural selection is thought to have started. Maybe because of people's fascination with fossils and the sequence of species development on earth. Maybe because it seems easier to understand than the new, mathematically oriented study of the origin of life. Or maybe because human beings are fascinated with the idea of apes becoming men. Whatever the reason, it seems that virtually everyone places most of the emphasis on this final step of "molecules to man."

Now that scientists can understand the extreme improbability of the first step alone, problems for evolutionary theory are only multiplied as we approach the final step. And when we analyze evolution and intelligent design in regard to this step (see chapters 12–15), we'll find that there is just as much difficulty in getting through this stage as with the other four.

Is the Bridge Falling?

If a single component of the evolutionary bridge is broken, the theory fails. That component could be

- the development of the very first bacterium—which requires at least *100,000 base pairs* of DNA, precisely assembled—or

- the proliferation of more than *1.7 million species*—many with billions of base pairs of DNA, all precisely developed and organized—or

- the ultimate development of man—with *3.2 billion base pairs* of DNA—all precisely formed and assembled.

Even scientists trying to explain evolution admit aspects of the theory are impossible. For example, in their book *The Origins of Life,* evolutionists John Maynard Smith and Eors Szathmary acknowledge,

> The first replicating molecules, whether nucleic acids or something simpler, could not have specified anything, and so could not be said to carry information. They are best thought of as replicating structures.[5]

In other words, it seems that the first building blocks of life could not have acted as vehicles for information! And we've already seen that the *source* of new information that increases complexity is a puzzle for evolutionary theory. Then the mathematical improbabilities increase vastly when more complex cells and organ systems are said to have developed.

But perhaps the most amazing advent of the supposed evolution scenario comes when more complex cells start developing into highly complex creatures of many different types with many different DNA characteristics and organelles (that is, "organs within the cell")—all within a relatively short period of time. In later chapters, we will look more closely at the improbabilities that are exposing the breaks in the bridge of evolution.

Questions that Need Answers in Order to Keep the Evolutionary Bridge from Falling

1. Could the proper atoms come together at precisely the right time and place?

2. Could the right molecular orientation (chirality) come about to effect "workable bonding"?

3. Was there enough time to randomly assemble even the first cell?

4. What alternative process could have created a cell nonrandomly?

5. How was life infused into the first cell?

6. How could a cell reproducing by binary fission change into a more complex cell?

7. Where did the information come from to increase cellular complexity?

8. What mechanism caused the changes from one species to another?

9. How could highly complex systems form gradually if all their parts are necessary for the system to work?

10. Was there enough time to change simple cells into more than 1.7 million highly complex species?

Part 2

A Look at the Bridge's Components

Three

Hard Evidence Versus Soft Evidence

When you think of something hard, you think of something firm. It doesn't give way. It's like rock beneath you. You can trust it to be stable.

Good bridge design involves calculations of the amount of stress put on every one of the bridge's critical components when a weight is applied. If any single critical component fails to withstand the applied forces, the bridge fails.

Because the design of bridges is based on hard calculations, which in turn are based on many experiments on the strength of different materials and structural designs, we can trust the outcome of the design to a very high degree of certainty. Engineers rely heavily on lab testing, experimental physics, mathematically proven formulas, and statistics in developing successful designs. Key to the conclusions they draw is *probability analysis* of experimental results.

In the scientific world, hard evidence is gained by similar means. However, many people simply assume that "science is science." They think that all sciences are the same in their use of evidence. But nothing could be further from the truth. Webster's dictionary has many definitions of science, ranging from the strict: "knowledge...gained through experience," to the very broad: simply "observation."

Let's look at the key words in these definitions. *"Experience"* in science is normally gained through experimentation. A hypothesis is formed. A test is devised that can test the hypothesis to see if it consistently predicts results (generally using statistical analysis). Conclusions are then drawn, based on the test results. *"Observation,"* on the other hand, is simply a systematic study of something. Observational studies can lead to statistical verification, but often they do not.

Experimentation according to the scientific method leads to *probabilistic* (statistically reliable) results. Observation, on the other hand, may be very valuable, but it may also lead to conjecture and speculation.

An Example

Suppose we want to evaluate something like the chances of safely driving a heavy truck across a bridge we're going to build. We could use a hard-science approach or a soft-science approach. Going back to our alternative bridge designs on page 13, we might come up with two methods:

- *Bridge 1, using hard-science analysis.* Engineers design a bridge that crosses a wide channel using a slender steel I-beam truss. The design is based on analysis of and experimentation with I-beam and truss construction. Calculations are made for tension, compression, torsion, and deflection upon all key members of the bridge. All calculations are based on lengthy experimental testing of the strength of steel under various loaded conditions.

- *Bridge 2, using soft-science analysis.* Architects design a massive slab bridge consisting of nonreinforced concrete to cross the same wide channel. Their observation of Roman structures has led them to believe that a massive concrete design is the best one. It looks far stronger than the truss designed by the engineers because of the bulk of the concrete. But its design is based only on the observation that concrete is thick, heavy, and seems strong.

Which bridge would you cross with a very heavy truck?

As we noted earlier, the great mass of nonreinforced concrete is probably *far less* safe because concrete is not strong in tension (on the bottom) when weight is applied. It may not even be able to hold its own weight (depending on many factors—width of the span, dimensions, and so on). On the other hand, a properly designed I-beam steel truss, though appearing relatively weak, can withstand considerable weight. In our example, the engineers used hard science—strength calculations based on physics, research, and experimentation. The architects used soft science—observation.

Things are not always the way they appear.

Hard Evidence

Most hard evidence involves mathematics. Using mathematics, experiments can be set up to measure and calculate all kinds of things: weight, height, width, depth, speed, acceleration, and so on. When experiments are devised that produce measurable results, those experiments can be repeated. If, upon repetition, results can be predicted with a high degree of certainty, typically an equation is established to mathematically define the relationship of the factors involved. Such an equation becomes hard evidence for evaluating future events that have the same characteristics as the event that was already tested experimentally. Engineers use such equations routinely for design of new structures.

Probability and statistics are major ways in which mathematics is used in the hard sciences. If the results of an experiment offer a very high degree of statistical consistency, then we have a high degree of "hard" precision in the evidence.

For example, consider dropping an apple numerous times and calculating its rate of fall. Such an experiment could lead to acceptable scientific laws of gravity and motion because of its extreme predictability. Or consider calculating the path and motion of the sun and the moon. Accurate measurement and computation leads to a precise prediction of the dates and times for solar or lunar eclipses. Finally, consider flipping a coin 1000 times. Experiments and probability indicate that the number of heads flipped will be very close to 500. Also, probability can be used to falsify a hypothesis. If an event is demonstrated to have enormous probability of not happening, it is deemed impossible by statisticians.

Hard-science experiments and calculations have led to the laws and formulas of physics, thermodynamics, chemistry, and engineering—all hard sciences, and all extremely predictable. These are the sciences that allow us to build bridges and buildings with confidence, knowing they are structurally sound. These are the sciences that allow us to land men on the moon or launch space probes that travel immense distances predictably. And these are the sciences that allow us to make refrigerators, microwave ovens, and medicines. Every day, we plan our lives in accordance with the hard sciences. Think about it. Every time we drive a car, go over an overpass, go up an elevator, drink treated water, or take medicine, we are placing our lives in the hands of what hard science has learned.

Probability

Probability is calculation of the odds of the random occurrence of an event or series of events. The easiest and most familiar example of *probability analysis* is the simple coin flip. We know one side is heads and one is tails. We know, therefore, that the probability of "heads" on a single flip is 50 percent or $1/2$. So what is the probability of flipping two heads in a row? The mathematical definition requires us to multiply the probability of the first event by the probability of the second. So the probability of two flips of heads would be $1/2 \times 1/2 = 1/4$, which is the same as a 25 percent chance. We can see how quickly the likelihood of multiple consecutive flips of heads is reduced when we consider a few more examples. The probability of seven consecutive heads is less than 1 chance in 100 (that is, $\frac{1}{2}$ x $\frac{1}{2}$ x $\frac{1}{2}$ x $\frac{1}{2}$ x $\frac{1}{2}$ x $\frac{1}{2}$ x $\frac{1}{2}$ = .78 percent). The probability of ten consecutive heads is less than 1 chance in 1000.

Another common example of relating probability to real life is the random chance of someone winning a typical state lottery with a single ticket. The probability of that happening is about 1 chance in 10,000,000.

Rather than writing out "1 chance in 10,000,000 (10 million)," scientists have accepted a standard called *scientific notation*, which assumes base-ten numbers with an exponent attached. Don't worry about the fancy math terms—this essentially means that the above probability for winning a state lottery would be written "1 chance in 10^7." In other words, the *exponent* "7" corresponds to the number of zeros after the 1. As we've already seen, 10^7 is a very large number.

The numbers we will be dealing with in this book are sometimes so incredibly large that only by relating them to common events (such as coin flips or state lotteries) can we appreciate how huge they really are.

Sometimes people want to reject probability as a means of proving (or disproving) an event. However, we need to keep in mind that we live with probability every day, even every second, of our lives. What is the probability that we'll be alive to take our next breath? That we won't have a heart attack? That we won't be struck by a meteorite? That our car will start? That we will close the sale? The list goes on and on.

Here are some examples of some approximate probabilities we face every day:

- the chances of dying from heart failure today = 3 in 1,000,000 (3 in 10^6)

- the chances of dying in an auto accident today = 1 in 1,000,000 (1 in 10^6)

- the chances of being killed by lightning this year = 1 in 1,000,000,000 or (1 in 10^9)

- the chances of winning a state lottery (per ticket) = 1 in 10,000,000 (1 in 10^7)

- the chances of dying in a plane crash this year = 2 in 1,000, 000,000 (2 in 10^9)

Even things we assume are absolute facts have been analyzed experimentally and given a probabilistic outcome. Consider gravity, for example. It is tested and demonstrated every day. However, there is still some incredibly low probability that it might not always hold.

———————

Let's return to the coin flip example to attempt to relate to some truly large numbers, the kind that we'll see in some of the hard-science calculations in following chapters. What is the probability of flipping 150 heads in a row? The math is fairly simple—just multiply $\frac{1}{2}$ times itself 150 times. The bottom number of the fraction becomes so large that straight calculation is difficult for some computers. Using logarithms, this number can be calculated as follows:

$h = 2^{150}$

$\log_{10}(h) = 150 \times \log_{10}(2)$ [because log (h^n) = n x log(h)]

$\log_{10}(h) = 4.5$, so…

$h = 10^{45}$

In other words, the probability of flipping heads 150 times in a row is 1 chance in 10^{45}—or 1 chance in a billion trillion trillion trillion!

A skeptic might say, "Well, the probability is still not zero—it *could* happen." Let's try to understand how unlikely the event of flipping 150 heads in a row really is. Assume you could convince 150 friends to join you in a gym for a coin-flipping experiment. Assume further that each of you would flip a coin a second—all together, 150 flips per second. Of course this is no small feat. The time it takes to flip a coin, look at it, and see what everyone else has would certainly take far more than a second. However, let's consider it possible. Even if you and your friends could start flipping at the time the universe began (according to most scientists, 15 billion years ago), you would still only be able to flip 10^{17} times. After all that time, what is the probability that you would have succeeded in having one coordinated flip be all heads? It would still be only 1 chance in a ten thousand trillion trillion.

Dr. Lee Spetner looks at this example another way. He assumes that ultrafast computers could simulate 150 coin flips every trillionth of a second. Furthermore, he assumes that 10 billion of these computers could be made and managed (assigning one or two to every person on earth). In his scenario, if the experiment were to be run for 3000 years, there would still be only 10^{42} trials, so the probability of one all-heads flip would still be only 1 chance in 10^3, or 1 chance in 1000.[1] Statisticians would argue that flipping 150 heads simultaneously (or in a row) is impossible for all practical purposes.

In evaluating what is required for evolution to take place, we will be analyzing events with *far less probability* than 150 simultaneous coin flips.

Probabilistic Proof

Scientists need a standard by which to gauge if something is possible or impossible. Otherwise, someone could unendingly claim that anything is possible, regardless of the amount of data and tests that support a certain conclusion. For example, even though gravity has been confirmed by experiment and by experience every day of our lives, a skeptic might still claim there's a chance it doesn't always hold. (However, I have yet to see a skeptic—a sane one, anyway—jump off a high cliff to prove such a theory.)

There is a limit beyond which something is for all practical purposes impossible, as in the coin flip example above. For probabilistic purposes, scientists generally regard anything with less than 1 chance in 10^{50} of occurring randomly as essentially impossible or absurd (without supernatural input). So in this book, when we look at the odds of evolutionary events taking place, we will use the same standard.

The hard sciences use mathematics, experimentation, and statistics as a foundation for determining a highly probable outcome. Evidence that is consistent with mathematical calculations based on proven formulas and data is the best, most solid evidence—and reasonable, useful assumptions can be based on such evidence. Hard, empirical evidence leaves the least room for speculation and interpretation. It can eliminate a lot of "fanciful thinking" by demonstrating that some theories based on observation alone are unreasonable.

Soft Sciences

Many recent scientific advances started with soft science: the latest oil finds, Teflon, microwave ovens, and the like. Soft science usually starts with an observation that leads to a hypothesis. The hypothesis is tested by subsequent observation, which is used to support or deny the hypothesis. But soft-science procedures can be like using educated guesses to find a result that may or may not be there. They can be based on suppositions.

"Soft evidence" is like a sponge. Much of it is good—it can "suck up water." But you can't rely on it for everything—it can't hold much weight over a span. For example, in the analysis of the fossil record, soft science would argue that because two creatures have similar structure and because one creature apparently appeared on earth after the other (all soft evidence), the prior creature was the ancestor of the latter one. Is there hard, empirical evidence to support this? No. Could the creatures have come about separately? Yes. Is the soft-science conclusion speculative? Yes.

Consider the sciences of geology, anthropology, and paleontology. Much work done in these sciences is soft and is based on educated guesses, which are in turn based on previously obtained knowledge. For example, the soft-science prediction of the location of an oil well may be weak compared to the hard-science prediction of a solar eclipse. Even though continued study will certainly improve the ability to predict where oil might be, geology will not be as reliable as the prediction of a solar eclipse or the calculation of how much weight a specified I-beam will support. This does not mean that soft evidence is faulty—it simply isn't as strong as hard evidence.

With adequate testing, soft science can border on hard science. For example, a large number of core samples that demonstrate a granite base of rock in a certain area may statistically reach a high probability level. This probability shows that the conclusion of "granite" is statistically accurate.

Because of the broad range of conclusions that soft science often draws, and because of the varying validity of the evidence it relies on, soft-science conclusions must be carefully evaluated. For instance, one of the problems of the soft sciences is that simple observation can lead in the wrong direction. There was a time, before astrophysics, that humans looked around themselves and saw that the earth seemed flat. Their conclusion was that the earth *was* flat. Likewise, ancient soft-science astronomers, without the benefit of today's tools, concluded that the sun revolved around the earth because they observed it rising in the east and setting in the west.

When we turn to evaluating the origin of life, we should not equate soft-science "general biology"—based on observations—to hard science, based on calculations. Today we have the benefit of the hard science of molecular biology. We also have the hard science of astrophysics, which has now defined limits for the age and size of our universe. These and similar hard sciences provide important boundaries in evaluating what is possible in regard to the origin of life.

Examples of Soft-Science Conclusions About Origins

Soft science has been used for years in teaching evolution in public schools. As mentioned previously, some of the soft-science observations that are said to be evidence for evolution include the following:

- *Commonality of body parts* between different species. Evolutionists contend that such similarity is evidence of a common ancestor for those creatures.

- *Commonality in embryos* at a certain stage of development. It is said that this may indicate a common ancestor.

> *Commonality between the DNA of all species*, along with the observation of differing species in various fossil layers, has led to the conclusion that complex organisms developed from more primitive life forms.

As we more thoroughly examine these and other claims in the following chapters, again and again we'll see that such observations fail to provide solid parts for the bridge of evolution. The fossil record, so highly regarded by many, has failed. Logic and intuition have failed. And the hard-science world of physics has certainly failed evolutionists. Now the greatest frontiers in the study of origins—molecular biology, astrophysics, and probability analysis—are doing the same.

Although some dedicated evolutionists are still searching for reasonable hard-science answers, the theory of evolution can no longer pretend to rely on hard science. Instead it relies on unsupported speculation or falls back on outdated soft-science ideas. Nonetheless, new evidence that makes evolution implausible is not taught in our schools yet. Rather, evolution continues to be strongly taught in our educational system. We should ask ourselves this question: Why?

Evolution Is Assumed to Be True

Unfortunately, we live in a society where evolution is assumed to be fact. Throughout my research of literature written by evolutionists, I found that conclusions were drawn based on the starting assumption that evolution was fact. Various theories were then considered to see which one best fit the "fact" of evolution. In such cases, evolution itself was never questioned. It was never suggested that intelligent, supernatural design might actually be a more reasonable theory and have more evidence to support it. The assumption that evolution is fact has held sway for decades, and it will only change as scientists choose to promote the facts that are now abounding from hard science. (For example see chapter 15, "Intelligent Design and Information Theory.")

A Closed System of Thinking

Recently I reviewed a textbook designed for sixth graders entitled *Earth Science*. It was published in 2001 and endorsed by the National Geographic Society. Peppered throughout the text was the presupposition of evolution:

> Plant life evolved on land.[2]
>
> By this time, animals began to move onto land with the plants.[3]
>
> Birds evolved from dinosaurs.[4]
>
> Fossil evidence shows that ancestors of the present-day whales and dolphins once lived on land.[5]

The point is that children are indoctrinated that evolution is a fact. And now, well over a hundred years of indoctrination has already established many people's thinking—in spite of new evidence. It is only because of these many years of presupposition that evolution remains in textbooks. It keeps perpetuating itself like this:

1. People want to know about the origin of life.

2. People go to those who are thought to be experts (evolutionists).

3. People are told the evolutionary theory, modified a bit since Darwin's time.

4. Nobody questions the "experts." Evolution becomes entrenched in the educational system.

An example of this is a cover story in *Time* magazine from October, 1996. Robert Wright states in his article "Science and the Original Sin,"

> As a story of creation, the book of Genesis long, long ago crumbled under the weight of science, notably Darwin's theory of natural selection.[6]

The Facts Are Coming to Light

However, as we saw in chapter 1, even convinced evolutionists recognize that neo-Darwinism is nothing more than a theory—even though they assume that it is a fact. They repeatedly describe theoretical changes using words and phrases like "maybe," "possibly," "we think that," "if," and so on. In fact, not a single one of the critical transitional steps identified by evolutionists has any strong evidence—which is admitted by evolutionists themselves (see chapters 7 and 8)! This hardly sounds like a theory that has logically crushed theories of supernatural creation, such as intelligent design.

Today, evidence from modern hard science is enabling scientists like biochemist Dr. Michael Behe, astrophysicist Dr. Hugh Ross, and mathematician Dr. William Dembski to counter outdated thinking. We are seeing changes in the way the evidence is viewed. In fact, the common presupposition that evolution is right may soon be behind us.

four

Observation: Examining Things Logically

Though most of this book deals with hard evidence, there is some soft evidence that we should still consider. This evidence is based on straightforward logic. For example, a missionary once told me he had explained the concept of evolution—that man had descended from apes—to a group of natives living in the Amazon. He was immediately greeted by roars of laughter. They couldn't understand how anyone would believe such a thing.

Today we have DNA technology, other findings from molecular biology, and much other evidence that indicates that the natives' laughter was well-founded. But let's take a closer look at the logic displayed by the natives. We should not dismiss the simple process of observation (yes, soft science) that made them laugh.

Random or Created?

The example of the Amazon natives illustrates something that has been apparent throughout human history. Human beings, having a mind, can readily recognize whether something is created or occurred by random chance. Something created, designed, or built has a form that defies randomness. It appears to have a purpose. Think of Stonehenge. In essence it's simply a collection of rocks. But the careful shaping of the rocks, their placement, their consistency in size, and their pattern leads us to recognize that the rocks did not accumulate by accident. They were shaped and placed intentionally, though we can only speculate as to how and why.

Likewise, imagine that you're taking a walk in the desert. You might step over hundreds of stones, here and there kicking one away. Suddenly one "stone" catches your eye. It has obviously been purposely shaped. After a moment, you recognize its form as an arrowhead. There is no doubt in your mind that it is something that was created. It has a form. It apparently has a purpose. And it is normal and intuitive to reach that conclusion.

As a further example, consider the "Monkey Face" rock formation on Smith Rock, at Smith Rock State Park in Oregon.

Courtesy of Oregon State Parks and Recreation Department.
Contact: www.oregonstateparks.org or 1-800-551-6949.

When you look at it, the rock does resemble a monkey. But was it purposely created? No. It's obvious to any observer. You could call the rock "gorilla rock," or "dinosaur-head rock," or many other things. Does it glorify monkeys? Or was it just randomly formed and happens to look like a monkey's head? (Today many rock climbers love to climb Smith Rock, but it wasn't created for that purpose.)

Now, consider another rock, one that we all recognize, Mount Rushmore.

This "rock" was obviously created. In fact, it's a rock that's been turned into a monument. It took purposeful energy and design to create it. And it has a clear purpose—that of honoring four great presidents.

The above example demonstrates how natural it is to see the difference between created things and randomly developed things. And so far we've only dealt with simple rock formations.

The Systems Inside Living Beings

Dealing with a design in rocks is simplistic compared to the complexities of life. Let's take our comparison a step further. Imagine that you've landed on another planet. You encounter a robot-like creature with multiple parts. Perhaps it has headlight-like "eyes." Maybe it has numerous steel-lever "arms." And you notice that it rolls around on a complex set of wheels that can be raised and lowered to fit the terrain. You would intuitively know that the robot had been created. In fact, you would recognize that human beings have been able to create such things.

Yet, for instance, the same types of motors that would be used in such a robot are found by the trillion in the human body. They have the same basic parts—but they're 200,000 times smaller than a pinhead. (See chapter 9 for more information about these "ATP motors.") Every cell in our body has hundreds of these motors. And in terms of efficiency, at the center of the motor is a wheel that turns at about 100 revolutions per second.[1] Today's molecular biology has made it even easier for us to understand we have been created by some incredibly intelligent designer, now that we can investigate the amazing biological machinery we can't even see.

All this is nothing new. In ancient times people would notice the intricate details of a flower—all the minute, complex components. Or they would observe a centipede—so small, yet so complex. Looking at more complex creatures, they would ask, how did all the body parts seem to "know" how to form themselves together? How did they "know" where to go? How did they "know" how to diagnose and repair themselves? How did they "know" how to grow? How did these creatures "know" how to reproduce? The questions go on and on. Even on the "macroscale" of complete plants and animals, their complexity and design has been obvious for millennia.

Let's look at one more example gained from the recent major advances in molecular biology: the amazing harmony of the "factory system" of a human cell. Gerald Schroeder, who holds a PhD from MIT, describes it this way:

> Other than sex and blood cells, every cell in your body is making approximately two thousand proteins every second. A protein is a combination of three hundred to over a thousand amino acids. An adult human body is made of approximately seventy-five trillion cells. Every second of every minute of every day, your body and every body is organizing on the order of 150 thousand, thousand, thousand, thousand, thousand, thousand, amino acids into carefully constructed chains of proteins. Every second; every minute; every day. The fabric from which we, and all life is built, is being continuously rewoven at a most astoundingly rapid rate.[2]

It defies logic to pretend that such complex systems—systems that work together in such a precise and harmonious way—came about randomly. It is plainly absurd.

Stories About First Life

As a final illustration of the power of intuitive analysis, let's consider the logic of two stories about the development of first life.

Hans, the Watchmaker

Hans created timepieces. As a young man he made ordinary sundials. Later on, he built water clocks and hourglasses. And he fashioned all other kinds of clocks: magnificent grandfather clocks, pretty little anniversary clocks…clocks of every shape and size. But his most prized creation was a gold watch.

Hans worked on the details of his gold watch for many years. Day after day he labored over its design—sizing every gear, calculating every tiny weight, exquisitely detailing the artwork. Meticulous care went into the manufacture of each part. Tiny gears were microscopically measured, formed, and polished for precision. The balance wheel was carefully calibrated to ensure maximum accuracy. The spring, the casing, the face, the crystal…every detail was crafted to create the most perfect timepiece ever.

Finally, when the last gear was delicately placed, the polished crystal gently set, and the gold chain lovingly attached, Hans marveled at the beauty and precision of his masterpiece. But then he realized he was still holding just a beautiful ornament. He began to wind the watch. The sound began: *tick, tick, tick.* And the ornament had become a timepiece.

Evolution, the Watchmaker

Billions of years ago, the earth was far more favorable to manufacturing than today. Covering the planet was a sea of "ooze," richly laden with the exact elements needed to create timepieces. Bits of gold, bits of silica, even bits of paint.

Years and years went by. Then the inevitable happened. Bits of metal were joined together by volcanic heat. Amazingly, the molecules of metal bonded in the exact way needed to build intricate gears and balance wheels. As the parts tumbled in the ooze, delicate polishing occurred—polishing precise enough to produce a perfectly calibrated timepiece.

Millions of years went by. Molecules of black paint came together in exactly the way needed to make numbers. And they coincidentally landed on a surface randomly covered with pure white paint. Amazingly, nothing eroded in all this time. As years continued to pass, eventually the gears, the wheels, a face, a crystal, and a beautifully engraved chain came together to form an exquisite gold watch. It was a product of exactly the right mix of materials—and billions of years. It was beautiful. It was complete and meticulously formed. It was perfect in every way...almost. It still needed someone to wind it.

Although we will be discussing mathematical analyses later in the book, this chapter, and particularly these stories, demonstrate that it doesn't take a "math whiz" to understand that the bridge of evolution is flawed. Knowing that there was no "watch-winder" is enough by itself. In fact, from observation, intuition, and logic alone, there is adequate evidence for the intelligent design of living things.

Five

The Myths of Evolution

"He's got a long gray beard and wears a bright red suit," my father said. "And he laughs all the time because he's so happy to deliver toys to all the children in the world. In fact his tummy jiggles because he's so fat. Guess what else...he travels in a sleigh pulled by reindeer—at night on Christmas Eve. He comes down the chimney when everyone is asleep to bring presents to all the boys and girls who've been good."

"Why does he do that, Dad?" I asked.

"I dunno. I guess because he just likes little kids," my father replied.

"What happens if kids are bad?" I asked.

"Oh, he puts awful, black coal in their stockings," my dad emphasized.

"Have I been good?"

"So far," Dad said. "Just keep it up and I'm sure you'll be fine."

Myths are part of our culture—and every culture. Not only are we inundated with children's myths about Santa Claus and the Easter Bunny, but adults have always embraced myths—myths that try to explain mankind's origin, purpose, and destiny.

Probably the most common myths of all are the myths of how life came to be. Virtually every culture seeks to explain this in a frame of reference that humans can see and understand. For example, according to Norse myth, the giant Ymir and the cow Audhumla were the first living things, born out of melting ice. Audhumla's milk fed Ymir. As the cow licked the ice for salt, it freed the body of Buri, the first man, who then begot a son, Bor.[1] Oddly enough, this Norse myth—and many myths about human origins—contain ideas that are similar to evolutionary theory:

1. Life can come from nonlife

2. Life can, by itself, bring about new forms of life

3. In fact, eventually animal life can develop into human life

There is now more than a century of evolutionary mythology that has permeated textbooks and the media. This mythology is essentially no different than the ancient myths of many cultures, except that today it is masked by the assumption that scientific discipline has been applied to it. For instance, when we examine the idea of *homology* (see below), we can see that it is the concept that Audhumla the cow was a predecessor of human beings.

Why do I make this point about myths so strongly? Well, the ideas I discuss on the following pages are taught in virtually all public schools. They totally convinced me when I was attending school. Then I started my research to see whether the bridge of evolution would really hold up. The following five areas of evidence turned out to be, not solid supporting members, but myths that could bear no weight at all.

Myth #1: Homology

Humans have elbows as do apes—meaning that both came from the same source. Apes have elbows like bats, meaning that apes descended from the same ancestor as bats. These are examples of *homology*—the idea that common body structures imply a common ancestor.

One of the "softest" of observational sciences came about by defining species through observation based on the principle of homology. In 1735 Carolus Linnaeus, a Swede, developed a system for classifying organisms. Essentially, it put similar-looking creatures into family groups, then into various subgroups. To a large extent this system is still used today. Linnaeus' work formed the basis of the development of the "evolutionary tree."

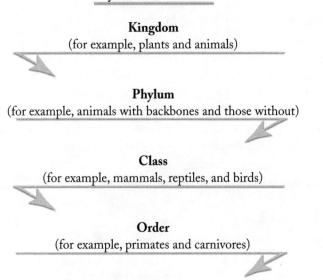

**The Species Classification
System of Linnaeus**

Kingdom
(for example, plants and animals)

Phylum
(for example, animals with backbones and those without)

Class
(for example, mammals, reptiles, and birds)

Order
(for example, primates and carnivores)

Family
(for example, dogs and cats)

Genus
(for example, wolves and coyotes are in the same genus)

Species
(members of a species can interbreed)

Darwin applied the species classification of Linnaeus, but he modified it to support his own thesis that the species all arose from a common ancestor. In *On the Origin of the Species*, he states,

> Such expressions as that famous one of Linnaeus, and which we often meet with in a more or less concealed form, that the characters do not make the genus, but that the genus gives the characters, seem to imply that something more is included in our classification, than mere resemblance. I believe that something more is included; and that propinquity of descent—the only known cause of the similarity of organic beings—is the bond, hidden as it is by various degrees of modification, which is partially revealed to us by our classifications."[2]

In essence Darwin was saying that, according to his theory, natural selection brought about evolutionary changes. But these changes left behind similarities, which Linnaeus and his proponents noticed. Since evolution is based on Darwin's concept of natural selection, it's not surprising that evolutionists now use such similarities—even such antiquated ones as those proposed 300 years ago by Linnaeus—as evidence for evolution today. But does it make sense? It's actually circular reasoning—we assume that commonality of body parts means common ancestors, because of a classification system that takes as its basis commonality of body parts.

Evolutionary Trees

When Darwin's model of natural selection became popular after 1859, evolutionists combined it with Linnaeus' system and developed *evolutionary trees* (combined with the "geologic column," discussed later) to define the "real path of evolution." Unfortunately, it was all conjecture—speculation based on the assumption that creatures with common body parts had a common ancestor. And it remains speculation today.

Think logically for a minute. Just because bats, chickens, dogs, and men all have elbows—does that truly imply that we came from the same ancestor? Isn't it more likely that a designer decided, so to speak, that "elbows work"? Might not such a designer decide to apply them to several basic types of mechanisms? For instance, a human design engineer might say something like, "Let's apply wheels to roller skates, bicycles, and cars—that system works for all those things." Sometimes we try to make simple things too complex.

Myth #2: The Processes of Microevolution Can Also Bring About Macroevolution

Evolution simply means "change" (in the sense of "unfolding"). "Naturalistic evolution" would then mean "change because of causes that occur in nature without man's involvement." However, the most common definition—the definition used in our school system—implies much more. It implies *the change of one reproducing species into another reproducing species.* Darwin's book *On the Origin of the Species* lays a reasonable foundation for the idea of natural selection (see page 69). But many biology textbooks take a major leap in the dark and also cite it as the foundation for the concept of interspecies evolution (*macroevolution*—see page 69). Let's look at a more precise definition of the terms we're concerned with.

Microevolution

Evolution (change) does occur within individual species. Perhaps the safest way to identify a species is by *genotype* (its genetic makeup). Some might identify a genotype as a reproducing species.

Considerable variety exists within the genetic structure of any species. For example, a human being may be blue-eyed, brown-eyed, have dark or light skin, be short or tall, fat or skinny…the list goes on and on. All of these potential variations exist within the human DNA encoding for an individual. As modern science has discovered, the "mapping," or the makeup, of the human genome is 3.2 billion base pairs of DNA. This information allows an enormous amount of flexibility for humans to adapt to their surroundings. This type of adaptation can be called *microevolution.* It has been observed and is accepted by virtually everyone.

This kind of change can occur within any species. One example of microevolution that has been commonly used in biology textbooks throughout the years has been the example of the peppered moth.* Peppered moths can be either black or white. In the area surrounding a village in England, a predominance of white peppered moths (98 percent) was noted at a time when light-colored lichen covered the trees. The white color camouflaged the white moths against the trees, while the black moths were more easily spotted by predators and were picked off and eaten. This increased the *gene pool* available for the white moths, which procreated more white moths. Later, as industrial pollution arrived, it killed the lichen on the trees, allowing the dark bark to be exposed. Now the black moths had a camouflage advantage and, through procreation, the proportion shifted to 98 percent black moths. Later, pollution was controlled, the lichen returned, and the moths shifted back to 98 percent white. What an amazing example of natural selection—"survival of the fittest"!

The problem is that such microevolutionary examples—which clearly demonstrate the remarkable adaptability *within* a species— are used in the broadest concept of evolution (from "molecules to man") to imply that natural selection can bring about change *between* species. That assumption is unfounded. In our example, nothing in the overall DNA structure of the moths changed. Yes, the proportion of color genes that was passed on clearly shifted due to the increased survival rate of the moth with camouflage advantage. But all this adaptation still took place *entirely within the confines of the species*. It would be tantamount to a gene pool shift in the eye color of human beings. Both options already exist within the vast human DNA molecule. If suddenly there became an environmental advantage for blue-eyed babies over brown-eyed ones, natural selection would logically cause that eye color to be passed on predominantly. But this does not mean a human can change into something else. And—to cite a typical example— microevolution has nothing to do with an ape turning into a man. Their DNA structures are totally different.

---

* There is now much support for the contention that some of the evidence for the peppered moth story was faked. See, for example, Jonathan Wells, *Icons of Evolution: Science or Myth?* (Washington, D.C.: Regnery Publishing, 2000).

Macroevolution

Neo-Darwinian evolutionary theory is based on the concept that one reproducing species can change into another. This process can be called *macro*evolution.

The idea of macroevolution is that species can change *between* genotypes through the process of natural selection. As I explained above, the peppered moth story is often used to imply that a new, better-adapted species somehow evolved because of a changing environment. Before we were able to recognize that DNA essentially *defines* a species, and that variations occur only within a well-defined pre-existing structure, a person who was relying on simple observation might have made the mistake of saying that the new color of peppered moth was actually a new and improved species. Such an observer might even have proposed that this improvement would eventually cause a peppered moth to become a bird, or something else. The historical contention has been that microevolution eventually leads to macroevolution. Many school textbooks still make that jump.

But now the evidence makes it clear that the peppered moth has always been the peppered moth, and always will be the peppered moth, regardless of how natural selection determines the "gene pool" for color. Today we can understand that leaps of improvement can happen in a species because it already has the capability within its existing DNA. But a species can be "improved" only "microevolutionarily"—in the sense of survival to meet circumstances. For another instance, bacteria that show statistically valid long-term variations in DNA structure (because their rapid procreation cycle allows for rapidly mutating populations—see chapter 12) still remain bacteria. *There is simply no evidence, even in this case, of a structural change in the DNA of bacteria that turns them into more complex organisms.* (The word "strain" is most appropriate to describe the changed varieties of bacteria.)

Natural Selection

The tendency for favorable genes to predominate in a species in order to allow the survival of the fittest has been termed *natural selection*.

Darwin was right. Natural selection is obvious. But it only works within a certain genotype. There have been many studies that demonstrate that gene pools favorable under certain circumstances survive and proliferate to help an *existing* species, as noted in the peppered moth example. But doesn't it seem logical that an intelligent designer would design such adaptability into any creation? Only an inept designer would engineer a mechanism that would fail if a single environmental circumstance changed—for example, if when lichen on trees suddenly died, peppered moths had been killed off entirely. Even human designs include compensating mechanisms—for instance, redundancy of systems in airplanes.

What about new breeds of dogs or new types of wheat? Don't these represent genetic changes that create new species? We have been able to tinker with existing DNA to actually improve some aspects of species through selective breeding. Some dogs seem more attractive as pets, wheat can become more abundant, and cows can produce more milk.

First, it should be noted that this is *artificial* selection, not natural selection. It really shows how an intelligent designer (in this case, human beings) has tinkered with a pre-existing process. Furthermore, the overall effect of such breeding is a *loss* of information in the DNA structure.[3] Such breeds generally need human support to continue existing. If left in the wild, these species tend to vanish through natural selection—in fact, extinction. In other words, people have "forced" variations within existing DNA for specific purposes (smaller dogs, higher yields of milk in cows, or greater yields of grain). But this requires *purposeful input*—intelligent design—to achieve those results.

We should also keep in mind that some kinds of artificial selection are actually *destructive*, such as inbreeding. Although inbreeding *may* pass on favorable genes, it is far more likely to pass on *unfavorable* genes, thus creating dangerous problems. To sum up, even the most careful crossbreeding doesn't create a new and different DNA structure. It simply can produce desired results by manipulating existing DNA.

Myth #3: The Evolutionary Tree and the Geologic Column

The idea that we can determine the evolutionary sequence of organisms based on the order of the appearance of fossils in geological strata (layers) has been part of evolutionary theory since the 1800s.

According to this concept, the *geologic column*—the layering of rock types—along with the fossils that are discovered in the layers, indicates the order in which plants and animals appeared on earth. This is often used together with homology (see page 64) to construct the evolutionary classification "tree."

Three key questions come up about the evolutionary tree and the geologic column:

1. Is there any scientific basis for the neo-Darwinian tree of life? Or is it simply arbitrary?

2. Does the fossil record support the tree of life? In other words, does it start with a few very primitive organisms from which others gradually appear over time?

3. Is the geologic column a trustworthy gauge of time to begin with?

Is the Tree of Life Scientific?

Although the tree of life enjoyed much support for many years, recent knowledge from molecular biology and analysis of species has called into question the idea that evolution followed the path shown by it. (However, textbooks have not yet caught up with this.) For instance, one of the twentieth century's greatest authorities on taxonomy is Harvard University's Ernst Mayr. In his standard text *Principles of Systematic Zoology*, Mayr admits that all categories such as *genus* and *family* are quite arbitrary, in that they seek to describe relationships that cannot be demonstrated experimentally among living populations. He goes on to say that

> no system of nomenclature and no hierarchy of systematic categories is able to represent adequately the

complicated set of interrelationships and divergences found in nature.[4]

Based on the above remarks, one would expect the neo-Darwinist Mayr to refute the idea of the evolutionary tree of life. However, in 1991, Mayr boldly stated,

> There is probably no biologist left today who would question that all organisms now found on the earth have descended from a single origin of life.[5]

In the ten years since Mayr made this statement, however, the support for it has been shattered. We'll consider the molecular problems in depth in chapters 9 and 10.

The Fossil Record and the Tree of Life

The second issue is whether or not the fossil record supports the concept of the evolutionary tree of life. Even in Darwin's day, fossil evidence had been uncovered of a vast "explosion" of life in what is termed the *Cambrian* period (see insert on page 83). This vast introduction of life included a broad variety of many fully formed phyla and classes of animals. Darwin himself was quite troubled about this. He observed in *On the Origin of the Species*,

> If numerous species, belonging to the same genera or families, have really started into life all at once, the fact would be fatal to the theory of descent with slow modification through natural selection.[6]

Although in Darwin's time, no earlier fossils were known, he hypothesized that earlier layers of rock had been changed enough by heat and pressure to destroy any fossils they might contain. Now, a century-and-a-half later, having the evidence of millions of fossils and considerable explorations of Precambrian rock, we know that this is not the case. Precambrian fossils have been found, but not the swarms of animals and plants Darwin had presumed would appear. Rather, only *single-celled organisms* have been found prior to the Cambrian period.

> Many paleontologists are now convinced that the major
> groups of animals really did appear abruptly in the early
> Cambrian. The fossil evidence is so strong, and the
> event so dramatic, that it has become known as "the
> Cambrian explosion," or "biology's big bang."[7]

The rapid appearance of many new life forms—all at the same period, as shown in the geologic strata, clearly contradicts the premise that a tree of evolution "grew" gradually from a single living cell. As Darwin himself pointed out, this fact is fatal to his theory. (We'll examine the fossil record in more detail in chapter 6.)

Can We Trust the Geologic Column?

The third issue in analyzing fossils in an attempt to map an evolutionary tree is the proposed geologic column itself. The concept of the geologic column is mostly based on observation. It is an attempt to assign an age to various objects (mostly fossils) found within various strata—usually sedimentary rock. Though it's found in many textbooks, the interesting thing is that there really is no single observable geological column.

How did it come about? Essentially, layers of rock were dated according to fossils found in them (*indexing* fossils). How then was the dating of the indexing fossils determined? It was based on the assumption that evolution was fact and that the tree of evolution was a useful guide to the sequence of fossil development. (This was previous to the development of radiometric dating, which was not utilized until 1910, and developed very slowly until the 1940s.)

Scientists now base the age of fossils upon the age of the rock they are located in. Substantial advances made in radiometric dating since the 1940s now enable us to date rocks to a high degree of accuracy. When fossils are embedded in rock that can be dated, their ages can likewise be determined. Also, when fossils are located between layers of rock, both of which can be dated, the age of the fossils can be assumed to be within the age boundaries established by the two layers. (See appendix B for more about radiometric dating.)

Myth #4: Embryonic Development Shows Similarities That Demonstrate Common Ancestry

Since Darwin recognized problems in substantiating his theory of evolution from the evidence of the fossil record and gradual changes, he hypothesized that evidence of embryonic similarities would support his claims. And indeed, the well-known drawings of embryos made by the German biologist Ernst Haeckel (1834–1919) seemed to show similarities between the embryos of various species. From the drawings, conclusions were made that supported Darwinian evolution.

Unfortunately, these drawings and conclusions were shown to be fraudulent. The fraud involved: 1) misrepresentation of the embryos prior to the drawings, 2) inconsistent selection of stage and age, and distorted drawing of the embryos, and 3) deception about which species were actually used. Haeckel was simply trying to support his own ideas.[8]

Myth # 5: The Miller–Urey Experiments Created Life in the Laboratory

Virtually anyone exposed to the teaching of biology in the past five decades has been told that, in 1953, Stanley Miller, along with his mentor, Harold Urey, developed a scientific means of simulating the earth's early environment and, within it, was able to create the "building blocks of life." This is enormously misleading.

First, these "building blocks of life" consisted of only a few amino acids—very far from the complex proteins, nucleotides, and organized information necessary for life. It is similar to manufacturing a drop of black ink and claiming you have created the building block for an encyclopedia (see chapters 9 and 10).

Second, Miller and Urey's simulation of the early-earth environment has been widely criticized. They artificially blocked out oxygen and "trapped" only the amino acids favorable to life. However, there is no way to explain how this could have happened on the early earth.

Third, it is almost never mentioned that the vast majority of components produced in these experiments were destructive "tar"—which would have *eliminated* any early life. The bottom line is, an impressive laboratory setup in biology textbooks has misled people into thinking that "science has created life." Nothing could be further from the truth.

———————

If the bridge of evolution is going to stand, it needs better components in its structure than the five traditional myths we've examined. Can we obtain better beams, anchors, and girders from some of the modern scientific disciplines? In parts 4 and 5, we will examine this question in detail. After all, if there is any truth to the claim of evolution, we owe it to ourselves to bring some hard evidence to the fore.

Six

The Fossil Record

The class rounded the corner giggling and jostling each other as they entered what promised to be the most interesting part of the museum. The guide told them they were about to see the history of man, and how modern humans came about.

They entered a darkened room with brightly lit dioramas containing models of human-appearing creatures, all of them engaged in various activities. There was a lot of pushing and shoving as each of the fourth-graders tried to get the best view of the first stop. Inside the glass-enclosed display was a group of relatively normal-looking people (not wearing many clothes, though). The adults were collecting berries, while the children appeared to be playing games.

"Okay, kids," the guide began, "these are some of your closest ancestors. They're called *Homo erectus* because they walked erect—upright. They existed as long as a million years ago and lived until about 300,000 years ago. They inhabited Europe, China, India, and Indonesia. One interesting feature of *Homo erectus* is that they had a brain capacity very similar to ours." The children paid little attention to what the guide said and were just laughing at the models' lack of clothing.

The group moved on, to the other exhibits—to the Neander-thal man window, to the Cro-Magnon window, and so on. Each display was greeted enthusiastically.

Finally they reached the last window, which showed some chimpanzeelike creatures. They were very hairy and looked as if they had come straight from the jungle. The younger chimps were wrestling and playing with each other, and the mother simply stood by, eating a banana. "Okay," the guide said, "this is the last stop in this room. These are your earliest human-type ancestors."

Josh started snickering, then couldn't contain himself any longer and broke out laughing loudly. "What's so funny?" his teacher asked. "You know you're supposed to be quiet in a museum."

"That can't be my ancestor!" he laughed. "My mom doesn't look anything like that! I think it's Brandon's great-grandma!" The whole class erupted in laughter, and the teacher smiled too.

An innocent comment, but perhaps it's relevant to our discussion. As I noted at the opening of this book, things aren't always the way they appear. Simply because an ape looks something like a human being doesn't mean they're related. (This gets back to the myth of homology—see chapter 5.) This is a point we must remember when evaluating the fossil record.

Ancient, fossilized bones and ancient creatures such as dinosaurs *are* fascinating. It seems like these remains can bring us closer to the way the earth really was long, long ago. But we must take great care in what we conclude from such soft evidence, keeping in mind that

- we are dealing with a soft science that is making speculative conclusions

- the fossil record is often evaluated starting from the assumption of evolution—which, as we've seen, is nowhere near a proven fact in truth, it is relatively easy to show that the fossil record *contradicts* evolution

The Crux of the Fossil Controversy

Many evolutionists claim that the fossil record confirms evolution. Others are embarrassed that it doesn't. Why is there this controversy?

Those who maintain that the fossil record confirms evolution all too often start from the assumption that evolution is a fact and then seek evidence to fulfill their belief. For example, they will search out similar-looking body structures and hope thereby to demonstrate that different species have a common ancestry. In reality this demonstrates nothing. An equally valid argument could be made that these species were created different and complete, maybe even at different points in time.

Think about it. Old human skulls are often used as examples of the evolution of man. This is very weak proof. Look at different skull shapes in existence around the world today. Sixty million years from now, someone could dig up Chinese, African, and European skulls and make that same mistake, hypothesizing that one was the ancestor to the other.

The assumption of evolution doesn't fit the model for good science. Instead, a valid hypothesis should be drawn first, carefully defining the parameters for its proof. For example, suppose it was hypothesized that fish evolved into frogs (an idea many evolutionists hold). Test criteria could then be established to see if the hypothesis could be fulfilled. For example, transitionary life-forms would be sought that had fins with stubs, and others, in which those stubs actually started to become legs. We would be looking for fossil evidence showing that the fish body started to take on the form of a frog. We might look for indications that gills were starting to turn into lungs. These kinds of scientific tests would help provide objective evidence of a change from fish to frogs.

The reason why so many biologists—whether they believe in evolution or not—don't think that the fossil record provides evidence for evolution is because all the organisms that make up the fossil record are fully formed and fully functional. We don't find lizards with small pieces of feathers starting to form on their scales. Fossilized life-forms either have feathers or they don't. We don't find organisms with only retina casings. They either have eyeballs or they don't. We don't find any with stubs for legs. They either have legs or they don't.

What Sort of Change Does the Fossil Record Show?

The fossil record actually shows that ancient specimens have forms virtually identical to nonliving life-forms. Here are some examples:

> The oldest fossils of land-dwelling animals are millipedes, dating to more than 425 million years ago. Incredibly, the archaic forms are nearly indistinguishable from certain groups living today.[1]

> The Florissant Fossil Beds in Colorado are internationally renowned for the variety and quantity (over 60,000 specimens) of fossils discovered. These fossils date to about 35 million years ago, roughly the halfway mark between the age of the dinosaurs and the first humans. The finds include over 1,100 different species of insects. According to the National Park Service's Geologic Resources Division, "the fossils indicate that insects 35 million years ago were much like those today."[2]

> A fossil dealer found fossilized jellyfish encased in about 12 vertical feet of rock, which, scientists say, represents a span of time of up to 1 million years. According to a Reuters article, "the fossilized jellyfish appear similar in size and characteristics to their modern brethren."[3]

If the fossil record confirms anything, it confirms the reality of little change. Plants and animals that existed millions of years ago are much like plants and animals today.

Is the Fossil Record Complete?

As we noted in chapter 1, Charles Darwin wrote in *On the Origin of the Species* that

> Natural selection can act only by the preservation and accumulation of infinitesimally small inherited modifications, each profitable to the preserved being.[4]

He went on to ask,

> Why, if species have descended from other species by insensibly fine graduations, do we not everywhere see innumerable transitional forms? Why is not all nature in confusion [he is talking about today's plants and animals] instead of the species being as we see them, well defined?[5]

Finally, he wondered,

> But, as by this theory innumerable transitional forms must have existed, why do we not find them embedded in countless numbers in the crust of the earth?[6]

At Darwin's time, we had unearthed relatively few fossils compared to the countless millions we have to analyze today. But the validity of his point hasn't changed. If the fossil record actually demonstrated evolution, we would have found "innumerable" transitional species showing infinitesimally small variations.

Today, researchers have concluded that the fossil record is virtually complete in what it has to reveal. For instance,

> A study in the Feb. 26, 1999, issue of *Science* combines data analysis of hundreds of early ancient mammal fossils with a mathematical model of evolutionary branching patterns to determine the completeness of the fossil record prior to 65 million years ago. The researchers concluded that the fossil preservation rate is high—high enough that the probability that modern mammals existed more than 65 million years ago

without leaving fossils is just .2 percent (two-tenths of one percent). Study author Christine Janis, professor of ecology and evolutionary biology at Brown University, proclaimed, "The fossil record for that period is good enough for us to say that those species would most likely have been preserved if they had been there."[7]

The Numbers Just Don't Add Up

Today, tens of millions of fossils have been unearthed and categorized. We have defined 250,000 distinct fossilized species. If true transitional forms existed, we should have at least the same number of transitional species—perhaps far more, given that many small changes would have taken place over time.

Even if we consider *punctuated equilibrium,* which theorizes sudden, abrupt evolutionary change and is a suggested alternative to the gradual neo-Darwinian model (see page 86), an abundance of true transitional fossils should still be present. And in line with neo-Darwinian theory, we would also expect the gaps between developing, diverging species to be small.

The numbers just aren't there, though.

- First, there are *no true transitional species* in the fossil record at all. (Only fully formed fossils with similar appearances are thought by some biologists to be transitions.)

- Second, *the rapid appearance of many separate, fully formed species*—in the *Cambrian explosion* (see insert on next page)—contradicts the gradualism proposed by neo-Darwinists. (It also confounds the molecular biologists who have to confront the questions of *irreducible complexity* and mutation through vast DNA change.)

In the intelligent-design paradigm, however, we would expect fully formed, fully functional creatures to suddenly appear. And naturally, there would be differences—gaps—between the various species. This is exactly what the fossil record indicates.

> **The Cambrian Explosion**
>
> During a very short period of time—thought to be from 525 to 550 million years ago—an incredible "explosion" of fully formed creatures appeared. Among them were more than 100 species of soft-bodied animals, an enormous number of small shelled organisms, and many others, such as the Burgess Shale arthropods. Scientists have named this period after Cambria, Wales, where large fossil beds were studied in the 1800s.

Paleontologists Speak Out

With so many fossils now available to view, and no real missing links having been found, evolutionists who are not committed to "making the evidence fit the theory" are speaking out. Some try to downplay the importance of the lack of transitional species. British zoologist Mark Ridley declares,

> The gradual change of fossil species has never been part of the evidence for evolution. In the chapters on the fossil record in *On the Origin of the Species,* Darwin showed that the record was useless for testing between evolution and special creation because it has great gaps in it. The same argument still applies...In any case, no real evolutionist, whether gradualist or punctuationist, uses the fossil record as evidence in favor of the theory of evolution as opposed to special creation.[8]

Interestingly, Ridley seems to echo what Darwin had lamented—the "gaps," or lack of fossils to be analyzed. As we've seen, this is no longer the case today, as pointed out by T.N. George as far back as 1960:

> There is no need to apologize any longer for the poverty of the fossil record. In some ways it has become almost unmanageably rich. And discovery is outpacing integration.[9]

Acknowledging the Gaps

Noted molecular biologist Michael Denton, who holds both an MD and PhD, examined the gap problem in his well-known book *Evolution: A Theory in Crisis*. The back cover of the book summarizes his views:

> Not only has paleontology failed to come up with the fossil "missing links" which Darwin anticipated, but hypothetical reconstructions of major evolutionary developments—such as that linking birds to reptiles—are beginning to look more like fantasies than serious conjectures.[10]

Even though some evolutionists attempt to use the fossil record to construct an apparent progression of plants and animals, the gaps cause this progression to fall apart, as evolutionary paleontologist George Gaylord Simpson observes:

> This [the gap in the proposed progression of horses] is true of all thirty-two orders of mammals....The earliest and most primitive known members of every order already have the basic ordinal characters, and in no case is an approximately continuous sequence from one order to another known. In most cases the break is so sharp and the gap so large that the origin of the order is speculative and much disputed.[11]

Simpson later notes,

> This regular absence of transitional forms is not confined to mammals, but is an almost universal phenomenon, as has long been noted by paleontologists. It is true of almost all orders of all classes of animals, both vertebrate and invertebrate. A fortiori [even more strongly], it is also true of the classes, and of the major animal phyla, and it is apparently also true of analogous categories of plants.[12]

It is not hard at all to find paleontologists who acknowledge that the many gaps in the fossil record essentially dismantle it as evidence for evolution. Here is a sampling of what has been said:

> Given that evolution, according to Darwin, was in a continual state of motion...it followed logically that the fossil record should be rife with examples of transitional forms leading from the less to more evolved....Instead of filling the gaps in the fossil record with so-called missing links, most paleontologists found themselves facing a situation in which there were only gaps in the fossil record, with no evidence of transformational intermediates between documented fossil species (Jeffrey H. Schwartz).[13]

> Despite the bright promise that paleontology provides a means of "seeing" evolution, it has presented some nasty difficulties for evolutionists, the most notorious of which is the presence of "gaps" in the fossil record. Evolution requires intermediate forms between species and paleontology does not provide them. The gaps must therefore be a contingent feature of the record (David B. Kitts).[14]

> A large number of well-trained scientists outside of evolutionary biology and paleontology have unfortunately gotten the idea that the fossil record is far more Darwinian than it is. This probably comes from the oversimplification inevitable in secondary sources: low-level textbooks, semi-popular articles, and so on. Also, there is probably some wishful thinking involved. In the years after Darwin, his advocates hoped to find predictable progressions. In general, these have not been found; yet the optimism has died hard, and some pure fantasy has crept into textbooks....One of the ironies of the creation–evolution debate is that the creationists have accepted the mistaken notion that the fossil record shows a detailed and orderly progression (cited by David Raup).[15]

> The record jumps, and all the evidence shows that the record is real: the gaps we see reflect real events in life's history—not the artifact of a poor fossil record (Niles Eldredge).[16]

> The absence of fossil evidence for intermediary stages between major transitions in organic design, indeed our inability, even in our imagination, to construct functional intermediates in many cases, has been a persistent and nagging problem for gradualistic accounts of evolution (Stephen J. Gould).[17]

Now that many evolutionists and paleontologists note the lack of fossil evidence supporting gradual evolution, what have they proposed in its place?

Punctuated Equilibrium

Developed in 1972 by Niles Eldredge and Stephen Jay Gould as a criticism of traditional Darwinism (gradualism), the theory of *punctuated equilibrium* holds that evolution occurs in "fits and starts"—sometimes moving very rapidly, sometimes slowly, and sometimes not at all. (As we've seen, Darwinism views evolution as a slow, continuous process without sudden jumps.)

Eldredge and Gould described the mechanism for punctuated equilibrium like this: Groups of creatures were cut off from the rest of their species in inhospitable fringe areas, where they could more quickly evolve. Such small groups allowed for inbred selection pressure that theoretically would cause positive (or negative) mutations to appear and be preserved—whereas in a larger population they would disappear. Such a changed species, it was further proposed, could eventually move into a broader geographical area, where individuals would become fossilized—thus giving the appearance of an abrupt change in the species. (It was argued that the original "fringe area" would never be dug for fossils.)[18]

However, punctuated equilibrium is really more of an observation—based on the fossil record, which shows sudden appearance of new species (for example, the Cambrian explosion) than it is a theory in the usual sense. And it still doesn't resolve the problems raised by the mutational process (see chapter 12 for more discussion):

1. Mutations do not add information.

2. Even if mutations could add information, there remains the statistical impossibility of a major macroevolutionary change.

3. Inbreeding has never been shown to do anything but *weaken* the long-term survivability of an organism.

But some evolutionists feel compelled to adopt the theory in order to account for the problem of the gaps:

> We seem to have no choice but to invoke the rapid divergence of populations too small to leave legible fossil records (S.M. Stanley).[19]

However, there has been a major ongoing debate among evolutionists themselves of the likelihood of the punctuated equilibrium model versus the traditional gradualistic one. It appears the traditional gradualism model still has strong support. The following cites a number of researchers whose writings have supported this view:

> It is now clear that among microscopic protistans, gradualism does seem to prevail (Hayami and Ozawa, 1975; Scott, 1982; Arnold, 1983; Malmgren and Kennett, 1981; Malmgren et al., 1983; Wei and Kennett, 1988, on foraminiferans; Kellogg and Hays, 1975; Kellogg, 1983; Lazarus et al., 1985; Lazarus, 1986, on radiolarians, and Sorhannus et al., 1988; Fenner et al., 1989; Sorhannus, 1990, on diatoms).[20]

Whichever model evolutionists choose to support, however, the lack of a single example of a real transition is evidence enough that the fossil record does not support evolution.

Plugging the Gaps

As we've seen, the fossil record yields support for evolution only when it's combined with speculation—and with the preconceived notion that evolution is fact. So searching out the fossil "missing links" is like trying to find pieces to a puzzle—but it's a puzzle that exists only in the mind of those who hold to evolutionary theory. What has resulted from the attempts to plug the gaps in the proposed evolutionary progression from simpler species to more complex ones?

The Archaeopteryx

Some evolutionists still point to unusual animals as missing links—for example, the archaeopteryx. This ancient creature has characteristics of both a bird and a reptile. For instance, it has wings covered with fully formed feathers. One of the discovered specimens has the type of sternum that would be necessary for wing-muscle attachment. Yet in addition, the archaeopteryx has teeth, claws on its wings, and a tail. Even the scientific community can't make up its mind exactly what the archaeopteryx is. Some view it as a missing link. Some view it as the first bird. Opinions vary.

However, we can be certain of one thing. It—along with other examples such as the Jurassic bird and *ichthyostega*, a type of ancient frog—doesn't fit the model of a true missing link, because all of its components are fully formed. Its wings are perfectly suited to flight, and the structure of its feathers is perfect to the smallest detail. Just because it contains some characteristics of different species means nothing. After all, humans share characteristics with crocodiles, such as the vertebrate eye—does that mean we are related to crocodiles? A true missing link should show partial development of something that appears fully formed later on.

A Recent Find Further Confuses Evolutionary Fossil Claims

On July 15, 2002, French paleontologist Michel Brunet officially announced his discovery of a hominid skull in Chad, Africa, dating to between 6 and 7 million years ago—nearly twice the age of the oldest current hominid fossil. The hominid was nicknamed "Toumai," meaning "tree of life." Henry Gee, paleontology editor of the magazine *Nature,* called the find the "most important fossil in living memory." [21]

What is causing enormous concern for evolutionists is that "Toumai" shows humanlike features much more "advanced" than several "intermediate" fossils in the supposed line of development of the human evolutionary tree. This find, along with many other hominid discoveries over the last ten years, has thrown out any clear path of human evolution, despite several decades of efforts to construct one. Daniel Lieberman, a Harvard specialist on human evolution, declared of Brunet's discovery, "This will have the impact of a small nuclear bomb." [22] In fact, some scientists say that these recent discoveries, especially that of "Toumai," may make it impossible to identify a true missing link.

Fascination with fossils is not a good reason to accept evolutionary claims about a progression of species development. As we've seen, the fossil record is one of the weakest parts of the evolutionary bridge.

But once we throw out preconceived ideas, these ancient specimens can open our minds to other alternatives that more reasonably explain the observations we make of them. Such an alternative is that different, independent species make use of similar, sometimes *very* similar, structures and parts—because they were designed that way.

Part 3

Another View of the Bridge

Seven

From Atoms to the First Cell

The class broke into laughter as I unveiled my "bridge" in our engineering design class. It wasn't very pretty. In fact, it looked like a bunch of toothpicks glued together. From its appearance, one would think it couldn't support anything, let alone the one-pound weight it was required to withstand. Nearly everyone else in the class had arrived with some version of an I-beam structure, in part because that was what we had been studying. I knew I was in for a big ribbing from my friends later on if my design didn't work.

This was the "test" day of our design competition. We were to design a structure that could span a specified distance using only balsa wood and glue. It was to support a static (nonmoving) weight of one pound, and we were given the dimensions of the weight. No other criteria were given.

This was an important project for two reasons: First, we were graded on it; and second, the class was extremely competitive and nobody wanted to lose or, worse yet, look foolish. Consequently, though we were all friends, nobody discussed their ideas or showed their designs to anyone else before the critical day.

Everyone arrived with their structures hidden in paper bags. Chosen by lot, one by one we had to come to the front of the class and present our design, along with the calculations that gave us reason to think that it would not only hold the weight, but also be the lightest and have minimum deflection (bending downward).

Some students presented structures that were overdesigned. They had virtually no deflection but were very heavy. Others had severe deflection, but used less material and were relatively light. As my turn approached at the end, I was somewhat apprehensive because nobody had taken the design approach I had. Although I had tested it, I began to question whether my bridge would work since I had tried to dramatically limit weight and deflection with a more complex design—that of a truss.

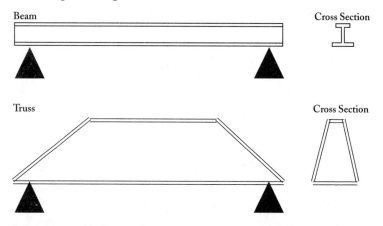

After I unveiled my structure, it was weighed. Its weight was found to be less than half of the next lightest design. Then I hovered over the truss and, holding my breath, ever so slowly applied the weight. It worked!

The next step was to measure the deflection. Because of the design, the vertical supports caused *torsion* (rotation) in the bottom horizontal supports. So I ended up with by far the lightest beam, with a *negative* deflection. Again, things are not always the way they appear.

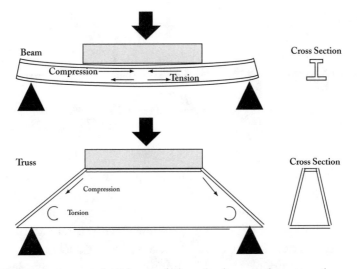

More importantly, I learned that the longer the span, the more complex the structure needs to be to limit weight and deflection while still having the necessary strength. A well-engineered truss can cross a longer span more efficiently than can a simple girder design. (The longest truss-bridge span in the world is located in Canada and is 1801 feet long, considerably longer than the longest prestressed-concrete girder span, which is 988 feet.)

The Span of the Evolutionary Bridge

Again, as we've seen before, the evolutionary problem is similar to the bridge problem. When the span to cross is as great as going from nonlife to today's worldful of complex creatures, it would require very strong and complexly interwoven evidence to support the weight of facts. Compare this to the problem of bridge engineering—a beam design would work to cross such a huge distance. Not even a truss design would be able to meet all the requirements. Engineers have found that the best design for long, deep spans is a suspension bridge. (The longest bridge span in the world is the Kobe–Naruto suspension bridge in Japan, with a length of 6532 feet. This dwarfs the 1801-foot longest truss span or the 988-foot longest girder-bridge span.)

Suspension Bridge

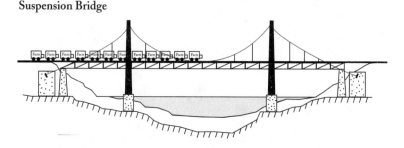

Suspension bridges have a more complex design than a beam or a truss, but they are far more efficient in crossing long, high spans. Their very strong cables can cross long distances, holding up a roadbed that's made of beams and stabilized with stiffening trusses. The load the cables carry is then transferred to the anchors, towers, and piers that support the cables. However, this added complexity also means there are more parts of the bridge that could fail. As we will see clearly, this is also the case with evolutionary theory.

In chapter 2, "Steps to Span the Gap," we made our first survey of what steps are needed for evolution to span the chasm between nonlife and all of today's complex life-forms. Now, in this chapter and the following one, we'll look at those transitions from the perspective of modern evolutionary theorists.

Even evolutionists struggle with how to explain these transitions at the molecular level, based on what we know today. To many of us, the evolutionary theory seemed to be a simple, strong concrete slab bridge when we were studying it in school. Now, based on the latest knowledge of biochemistry, it has taken on the vast complexity of the most intricate suspension bridge.

The Essential Transitions

Noted evolutionists John Maynard Smith and Eors Szathmary have outlined the major transitions required for naturalistic evolution to occur, in their book *The Origins of Life*. According to Maynard Smith and Szathmary, evolution can be broken down into eight very basic steps.[1] (In reality, of course, there would be countless trillions of steps over billions of years. Individual DNA molecules would have to experience countless macromutational changes—changes that would have to be passed on through countless generations—in order to account for all the varieties of species we see today.)

As a preface, let's keep in mind something that Maynard Smith and Szathmary themselves point out about the eight steps:

> Any one of them *might not have happened,* and if not, we would not be here, nor any organism remotely like us.[2]

Critical Transitional Steps
according to Maynard Smith and Szathmary

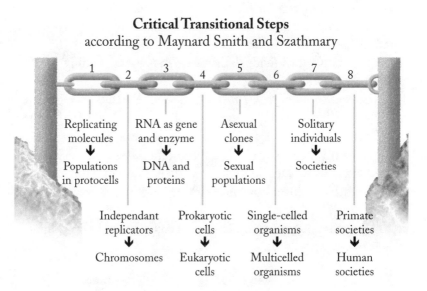

| 1 | 2 | 3 | 4 | 5 | 6 | 7 | 8 |

| Replicating molecules ↓ Populations in protocells | RNA as gene and enzyme ↓ DNA and proteins | Asexual clones ↓ Sexual populations | Solitary individuals ↓ Societies |

| Independant replicators ↓ Chromosomes | Prokaryotic cells ↓ Eukaryotic cells | Single-celled organisms ↓ Multicelled organisms | Primate societies ↓ Human societies |

Step I:
Replicating Molecules ➤ Populations of Molecules in Protocells

According to Maynard Smith and Szathmary, evolutionists presently think that the first step of evolution was the development of some kind of molecules similar to RNA. They would have been able to replicate themselves, but they would not have been capable of specifying (carrying information for) other structures. Maynard Smith and Szathmary also point out that there would have had to be different kinds of replicating molecules so they could "co-operate, each producing effects helping the replication of others." They also mention the need for some type of membrane or compartment to enclose the populations of these molecules.[3]

However, the idea of proper replicating systems of molecules is speculation, not fact. No evidence currently exists that indicates that their development is possible naturalistically.

Even though there was a type of replicating system developed in the lab in 1986, the system had *limited heredity* (limited ability to transmit individual characteristics to succeeding generations). For evolutionary development to take place as theorized, a system with *unlimited heredity* is required. Further, in regard to the simplest replicating system known today, Maynard Smith and Szathmary indicate that the system is "in a sense cheating." It works only because the right monomers (simple molecular ingredients) were supplied, along with a complex enzyme that "could not have existed on the primitive earth, before the origin of life."[4]

The authors sum up the existing evolutionary knowledge of step 1 by saying,

> For the present, we have to accept that the origin of molecules with unlimited heredity is an unsolved problem.[5]

Step 2:
Independent Replicators ➤ Chromosomes

A chromosome is a linked chain of replicating molecules *(genes)* that defines certain characteristics of the organism in which it exists. Even the simplest organisms must have at least one chromosome.

The chromosomal structure ensures that all the connected genes are copied together, thus preventing competition between genes within a membrane.

There are many specifications associated with the linking together of genes. They need to "make sense" in terms of the information provided to the organism. Their components must have the correct structure and chirality (see chapters 9 and 10).

Christian de Duve of the Institute of Cellular Pathology in Brussels, Belgium, sums up the current knowledge about step 2 this way:

> Little is known, however, of the manner in which these…compounds interacted further to generate increasingly complex molecules and molecular assemblages, up to the first living cells. To date, in spite of much experimental and theoretical work, a striking discontinuity still separates the most successful attempts at reproducing biogenic processes in the laboratory from the manner in which these processes take place in living organisms.[6]

To return to our illustration, would you be willing to drive a truck over a bridge that has a "striking discontinuity"?

Step 3:
RNA as Gene and Enzyme ➤ DNA Genes and Protein Enzymes

There are three basic molecular components to cells:

1. DNA molecules, which carry a species' "coded" information

2. RNA molecules, which copy and carry information for the development of the proteins needed for the organism

3. The proteins themselves

Evolutionists have suggested that, originally, not all three components were necessary, and that RNA by itself performed the function of both DNA and the required enzymes to produce proteins. The proteins produced are, of course, critical. In human beings, they make up the body's structure (skin, hair, muscle, and so on) and catalyze chemical reactions. If the suggestion about RNA were correct, it would require a critical step of evolution from the original process of RNA protein development to the current base sequence based on DNA, such as the one found in humans.

Again, however, Maynard Smith and Szathmary acknowledge that this evolution of the genetic code is little more than speculation in their own model. They comment,

> To explain its [the genetic code's] origin and evolution
> is a major challenge, which is just beginning to be met.[7]

When they propose RNA protein development as an intermediary step, the two scientists admit the speculative nature of the idea:

> We can only answer this question [that is, how a replicating system could evolve into today's "protein synthesizing machinery"] in vague outline.

They further add, "This outline is necessarily speculative."[8]

Other scientists have also suggested RNA as an intermediate step. They do this hoping to lessen the statistical problems of a theory that proposes that all the components of life come together at once (see chapter 11). However, all of these researchers acknowledge their uncertainty. In addition, they often address the magnitude of the overall problem. James Ferris of the Rensselaer Polytechnic Institute Department of Chemistry notes that

> no prebiotic simulation experiments have been reported
> in which polymers are formed directly from simple
> inorganic and organic starting materials.[9]

Ferris goes on to provide what he believes may be a plausible scenario for obtaining the needed catalysts for RNA development before the origin of life. Again, he provides no empirical evidence. He explains his investigations of RNA by saying,

> Problems exist with the proposed prebiotic [before the origin of life] synthesis of ribose from formaldehyde, as well as with other aspects of the prebiotic synthesis of ribonucleotides. These problems have prompted the search for simpler structures, similar to ribonucleotides, which may have been the basis for the first life on Earth.[10]

Dr. Robert Shapiro (PhD from Harvard, postgraduate work at Cambridge) has spent his life researching DNA and RNA. He takes a very firm stand against the speculation that RNA could have served as an intermediary in the development of the first cell of life:

> A number of scientists are advocating the idea that life began with an "RNA world" in which oligonucleotides catalyzed key reactions, including those needed for metabolism and their own replication. I have argued, in books and review articles, that this scheme is implausible on synthetic grounds: *the complexity of RNA is too great for spontaneous, unassisted assembly of the first molecules to take place.*[11]

We might conclude, therefore, that the third critical step in Maynard Smith and Szathmary's model of evolution is speculation at best and has, in fact, been criticized as being impossible.

––––––––––

Why do Maynard Smith and Szathmary see these first three steps as a prerequisite for the development of the first living cell? It's because continuing breakthroughs in molecular biology emphasize and re-emphasize the vast complexity of the cell. The three prebiotic (pre-life) steps that involve only chemical compounds seem to make the problem at least a little more manageable.

If evolution is going to survive as a theory, it needs to establish, at the very least, some evidence supporting the development of the first cell of life. Since such evidence is lacking, evolutionary theorists seem to be attempting to fit new theories to the answers that they want, not to the evidence.

Eight

From the First Cell to 1.7 Million Species

The bridge of evolutionary theory becomes more complex as it reaches further in the proposed line of the development of life. At the beginning of the last chapter, we saw that the more complicated a bridge design is, the more components it requires. With more components, there's a greater chance for the entire bridge to fail because of a flaw in a part. As we continue looking at the critical transitions necessary for evolution to have happened, can today's evolutionary scientists provide something stronger than the speculative notions we encountered in the last chapter?

At the outset, it's important to note that John Maynard Smith and Eors Szathmary do not include the critical step we looked at in chapter 2 (pages 29–33): How do self-replicating compounds just automatically cause "life" to appear within them? The question remains unanswered by them or by anyone else.

Further Essential Transitions

Step 4:
Bacterial Cells (Prokaryotes) → Cells with Nuclei and Organelles (Eukaryotes)

The critical first cell of life is believed to be a simple prokaryotic bacterium. The next important transformation is from a simple prokaryotic cell to a much more complex eukaryotic cell.

Prokaryotes are single-celled creatures that usually contain only a single chromosome and lack a defined nucleus. *Eukaryotes*—present in all other organisms—contain a nucleus that holds the chromosomes, along with a variety of *organelles*, which are like organs in the body (see chapter 9). Another very important difference between prokaryotes and eukaryotes is in the cell walls. Prokaryotes have a relatively rigid cell wall, which is an important part of the reproduction system because chromosomes need to bond to the cell wall. Eukaryotes, on the other hand, have no cell wall, so to speak. Instead they have a structural element called the *cytoskeleton*, which can maintain a boundary and perform a number of other functions.

The first major question that has to be asked is, how did replicating groups of molecules become the first cells? Maynard Smith and Szathmary propose that we "imagine" a system in which replicating molecules would "resemble an ecosystem." In this "ecosystem," they would compete for a limited supply of *monomers* (simple molecules with nonrepeating structures). They envision the replicating molecules both attacking and cooperating with other molecules to aid their chances of survival and reproduction. They also make two other assumptions. First, in order to increase possibilities for mutation, they believe that the "cycle of development" improved to cause eukaryotic cells to arise. They also assume that replicating molecules were enclosed within special membranes that "allow nutrients to pass through, yet are impermeable to macromolecules or smaller molecules that are involved in metabolism." Of all this, they acknowledge,

> Although we are still far from the artificial synthesis of such a system in the laboratory, this may happen in a few decades.[1]

Again, in the major transition from prokaryotes to the far more complex eukaryote-based organisms, evolutionists turn to theory and speculation to answer a critical question. Further, when Maynard Smith and Szathmary open their discussion of the commonly accepted hypothesis regarding development of organelles (the *symbiotic theory*), they note,

> Even if we accept the symbiotic theory of the origin of organelles, this does not explain the origin of the eukaryotic cell itself.[2]

The two scientists then try to explain the development of the cell itself with their own speculative idea. Again, the assumption of evolution is made, and the theory is designed around that assumption. In fact, their entire explanation of step four, as with the steps before it, turns out to be based on conjecture.

Ideas About the First Cell

It is commonly believed among evolutionists that the first living cell was a simple bacterium. There are several reasons for this idea:

- A bacterium is the simplest of any living single-cell organism. (Viruses are simpler, but they must invade another cell to become "alive.")

- The fossil record seems to show that bacteria are the earliest living organisms.

Every cell requires a source of energy. The options are

1. *photosynthesis*—energy from light— which is not possible at the origin of life because it requires complex and highly evolved proteins.

2. *heterotrophy*—energy from consumption of organic food—not yet present on the early earth.

3. *autotrophy*—energy obtained from inorganic sources, possibly from oxidation of hydrogen sulfide from hydrothermal (hot water) vents from volcanic outflows.[3] Some bacteria can survive by autotrophy, which would have been the only option on the early earth proposed by evolutionists.

Step 5:
Asexual Clones ➤ Sexual Populations

Prokaryotes (and some eukaryotes) reproduce asexually by cell division. At some point, evolutionists claim, a major transition occurred that allowed sexual reproduction between two individual eukaryotic organisms (see pages 37–38 to review information about this). According to evolutionists, this is an important step because sexual reproduction is thought to allow for a greater degree of mutation in populations. This would promote the kind of species diversification we see today. But how did this transition happen? Again, evolutionary scientists admit they don't really know. In introducing this part of their model, Maynard Smith and Szathmary note that "this transition is one of the most puzzling."[4]

The authors then provide a hypothesis of the transition from asexual organisms to sexual populations. This hypothesis involves a series of steps; Maynard Smith and Szathmary assume that these steps would be made simply because each one would benefit the "evolving species." There is no experimental evidence that the process is taking place. Rather, as before, it is simply based on the observation of certain organisms today and the assumption that evolution took place.

Uncertainty about this evolutionary transition abounds among evolutionists themselves. Maynard Smith and Szathmary observe,

> Because of these complications [the complexity of meiosis—the process of sexual reproduction in cells] and the obvious disadvantages associated with them, it is not surprising that the origin and maintenance of sex continue to be a matter of controversy among biologists.[5]

In this case, there is not even a single unifying theory about the transition. We continue to find nothing but flawed components in the bridge of evolution.

Step 6:
Single-Celled Organisms ➤ Animals, Plants, Fungi

This is the largest, most-discussed transition in the proposed progression of evolution. It involves change from small, unknown organisms to millions of plants and animals that we can readily see and study today. How did single-celled organisms change into multicelled creatures with millions of specialized cells (blood, hair, nerve, muscle, and so on)? How can single male and female cells *(gametes)* carry all the information necessary to develop into adult organisms with millions upon millions of cells?

Classical biology teaches that *positive mutations* account for the cellular changes necessary for evolution to take place. There are several problems with this hypothesis and they show up most obviously when we try to account for the development of all the species now in the world out of single-celled organisms. We'll look at the whole question of mutations in detail in chapter 12, but here's a quick summary of the problems:

- *Mutations are almost always destructive.* This is a well-known fact, acknowledged by Maynard Smith and Szathmary: "Most mutations reduce fitness."[6]

- *Even positive mutations have little chance of survival.* Noted mathematician and evolutionist Sir Ronald Fisher (one of the architects of neo-Darwinian theory) indicated that "a single mutation, even if a positive one, has little chance of survival."[7]

- *Multiple mutations have a multiplied chance of harming an organism.* This is because nearly all mutations are harmful.

In regard to step 6, Maynard Smith and Szathmary also attempt to explain the Cambrian explosion (see page 83), when millions of advanced creatures suddenly appeared. They also ask the question, if evolution was steady and continuous, how did many species appear at once, with no trace of them in earlier periods? The two scientists acknowledge that "we are left with a puzzle."

They then go on to suggest that some kind of environmental change caused broadscale mutations in more primitive "soft organisms." These soft organisms then disintegrated and left little or no trace in the fossil record, but the beneficial mutations were passed on to the organisms whose fossils appear in the Cambrian explosion.

As we will see in chapter 12, it is mathematically inconceivable that such diversity could happen naturalistically in such a short period of time. Yet again, we find serious weaknesses in the evolutionary claims.

Step 7:
Solitary Individuals ➤ Colonies with Nonreproductive Castes

The next major transitional problem that evolutionists encounter is how solitary organisms evolved into complicated societies. The three major societies that Maynard Smith and Szathmary describe are

1. ants, bees, wasps, and termites
2. some colonies of marine invertebrates (for example, corals)
3. human beings

It is especially those with nonreproductive castes—like ants, bees, and termites—that create an immense question for evolutionary theory. The main thing that differentiates these creatures from others is that there exists in them a reproductive division of labor.

For example, a hive of bees includes worker bees, drones, and usually one queen. Worker bees are just what their name implies. During their lifetimes, they successively clean the hive, feed developing bees, produce wax and build cells, guard the entrance of the hive and receive nectar, and finally hunt for food.

Drones are male bees whose sole job is reproduction. During mating they inject germ cells (sex cells) into the queen bee, which are stored in a sac in her abdomen. Queens may mate with many drones. When cold weather sets in, drones are generally pushed out of the hive to die.

Each hive must have at least one queen. The queen's job is strictly to mate and to lay eggs. After emerging from their cells, queens often fight for leadership of the hive, or one may leave and start another hive. The next job is a mating flight for the queen and drones. Upon returning, the queen spends the rest of her life laying eggs, one in each cell. If a germ cell is injected into the egg, it becomes a drone. Otherwise the egg develops into a worker bee.

Ants, wasps, and termites have similar societies and divisions of labor. They, along with bees, are all classed as *eusocial*. Eusocial creatures meet the following criteria:

- There is a reproductive division of labor (only one or a few individuals reproduce).
- There is an overlap of generations within the colony.
- There is a system of cooperative care of the young.

The puzzle for evolutionists has been, how did eusocial creatures develop the instincts to form and maintain colonies? One of the problems is the short time that the creatures survive. For example, most worker bees live only about six weeks in the summer or as long as a few months in the winter. Drones last only one mating season, and a queen's lifespan is limited to five years.

There arises a further question, given the evolutionary notion that competition and survival of the fittest bring improvement in a species. How did eusocial societies develop the instincts to *cooperate* instead of compete, especially in regard to most of the individuals supposedly giving up the right to reproduce?

Maynard Smith and Szathmary observe,

> The existence of non-reproductive castes, the so-called workers, in the social insects, and in some other social animals, poses a formidable problem to the theory of evolution, as Darwin already recognized.[8]

They, as well as other evolutionists, have proposed that genetic differences between individual castes of insects may account for a predisposition in their development. However, they are quick to point out that it must be a predisposition only, otherwise a colony might develop to contain only one caste.

Though there was some hope that understanding caste differentiation in colonies might lead to a greater understanding of how cells "know" which proteins to produce in the development of complex creatures, Maynard Smith and Szathmary summarize their conclusions about this transition of evolution as follows:

> As yet, the role of genetic predisposition in insect colonies is a matter of speculation rather than solid knowledge.[9]

Observations have also been made of instinctive behavior in many animal societies, not to mention human behavior, but conclusions also remain speculative.

Again we see evolutionary scientists themselves acknowledging the weakness of the theory. Again, the bridge of evolution continues to look shakier.

Step 8:
Primate Societies ➤ Human Societies with Language

The last major evolutionary transition proposed by Maynard Smith and Szathmary is the evolution of language. Language is called the "decisive step" in the transition from primate to human society.

First, the two researchers do note that some aspects of the human race—such as the tendency for balance within human society, including a division of labor—may be genetic. As evidence, they point to the eusocial organisms (ants, bees, and termites) that demonstrate this balance.

Then, say Maynard Smith and Szathmary, other social aspects of humans are obviously not genetic, such as beliefs and behaviors acquired from culture and environment. Examples include political and religious beliefs. All of these affect each individual's thinking and behavior.

Evolutionists maintain that these *learned* behaviors are different from *genetic* behaviors because they can be *horizontal* as well as *vertical*. To explain, genetic tendencies are transmitted only from parent to offspring (vertical). Learned behaviors, however, can move from parent to offspring, offspring to parent, or from any outside person to offspring (horizontal). Language is the key difference that separates humans from other creatures in this regard (though there is some degree of learning passed from adults to offspring in the animal kingdom).

Evolutionists point to the fossil record as possible evidence for the evolution of language. They indicate that supposed ancestors of humans—bipedal primates that made tools—had no evidence of language until about 30,000 to 50,000 years ago. At this time, evidence of cave paintings, personal adornment, burial of the dead, and trade indicates that language had emerged. Maynard Smith and Szathmary summarize the language problem presented by the fossil process thus:

> This raises several problems. Why the delay of 50,000 years between the appearance of the first anatomically

modern humans and the technical revolution? What selective force was responsible for the accelerated increase in brain size 300,000 years ago? When and why did language as we know it originate?

The problems are difficult, because a fossil skull can tell us rather little about the brain that was once inside it, and the stone tools little about the society that made them.[10]

Beyond the fossil record, how do evolutionary scientists answer the questions about the evolution of language? Often, they will point to "lower" animals that make different sounds when they see different threats in their environment. For example, vervet monkeys give out different cries depending on whether they see an eagle, a leopard, or a python. Presumably this signals other monkeys to climb a tree (when a leopard is sighted) or to go toward the ground (when an eagle is sighted). Evolutionists usually say that this proves there is some genetic link in terms of language development from more primitive creatures to humans.

However, other evolutionary theorists recognize the problem of drawing such conclusions from genetics alone. For instance, a computer simulation was designed by G.E. Hinton and S.J. Nowlan in which "neuronal switches" could be set either genetically or by learning. The switches had to be set properly to perform a desired action. The result is described:

If we depend on genetics alone, a population will never evolve the capacity to perform the action, because the chance that a genotype specifying all the correct settings will arise by chance is vanishingly small. Even if such a genotype does arise, it will be broken up by genetic recombination in the next generation.[11]

Unfortunately, for this final transition, we see factors similar to the seven steps before it:

- The observation of a similarity of human language to noises made by animals is used to reinforce evolutionary assumptions.

- Similarity of human social order to the social order of ants and bees is used to support evolutionary assumptions.

- There is no concrete explanation given for the mechanism for evolution.

An Evaluation of the Eight Transitions

The bridge of evolution is indeed complex—vastly more complex than the most intricate suspension bridge, and vastly more complex than was imagined even 20 years ago. The technical advances of the latter part of the twentieth century have allowed scientists to recognize the challenges to the evolutionary process at the molecular level.

Now that we are learning something about the multitude of components required, it's becoming clear that the anchors, piers, beams, cables—in fact, all parts of the bridge of evolution—are weak.

The eight transitions proposed by John Maynard Smith and Eors Szathmary share those weaknesses:

- There is a presupposition that genetic changes took place—a presupposition not based on empirical evidence.

- The theories that propose methods for the transition are not based on hard evidence. Further, they all have problems that evolutionary scientists themselves recognize.

- In summary, all of the transitional theories presuppose that evolutionary development is a fact, and they try to fit the evidence to that presupposition.

Part 4

The Micro:
Dismantling
the Old Span.
Building a
New One

Nine

The Complexity of Living Cells

What is the simplest form of life? A single cell. However, a single cell is extraordinarily complex. And all this complexity fits within a miniscule space.

A reproducing cell is the smallest living creature. Cells can vary in size from the smallest—bacteria, which are about 1/50,000th of an inch across—to the largest, the yolk of an ostrich egg.[1] There is also a wide variety in the shape and function of living cells (for example, cells for plants, or for muscle, blood, nerves, and so on). We can put the size of a cell in perspective by noting that about 1000 "average" cells would fit within the period at the end of this sentence. (And 25,000 bacteria-sized cells would fit in the same space.)

Despite the vast differences between them, virtually all cells do certain functions. These functions are so complex that a single cell is far more complicated structurally than the most modern factory in the world. All cells "breathe," eat, get rid of waste, grow, reproduce, and eventually die. They are essentially miniature animals—in fact, there are many single-celled organisms. (One of the most well known is the amoeba, often studied in biology classes.)

A Multiplicity of Parts

The true complexity of a living cell cannot be well appreciated until the individual parts of its structure are considered. There are a number of parts that are common to most cells. Take a look at the diagram below, which is a highly simplified representation of how a cell might be likened to a typical factory.

A Simplified Schematic of a Very Basic Cell

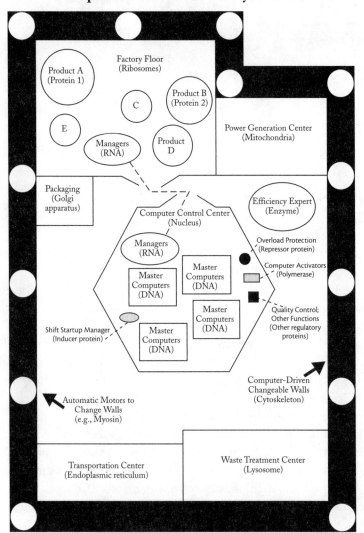

Below is a brief description of a few of the common parts of a cell. (Later in this chapter, we will illustrate how simplistic the factory illustration is when we review some of the intricacies of mitochondria, DNA, RNA, and protein chains.) Keep in mind, however, that all of this is packaged in a space usually a thousandth of the size of a period—sometimes less.

DNA is like the master computer—the essential part of every cell that dictates all its actions. Though an entire chain of DNA uses only six essential ingredients, the tiny chain is enormously long—often containing *billions* of parts. For example, if one were to take the amount of DNA in a single human body, straighten it out, and lay it end to end, it would extend for *50 billion kilometers* (from the earth to beyond the solar system)![2] Obviously the amount of complex information on a single strand of DNA is enormous. (We will dig into that complexity of information and its importance in later chapters.)

DNA is the primary element of chromosomes. Each species has a specific number of chromosomes per cell. For example, in humans, it's 23 chromosome pairs in "general" cells *(somatic cells)*, or 46 total chromosomes. Sex cells (also called *germ cells*) differ, in that their chromosomes do not occur in pairs (in humans, they have 23 *single* chromosomes). The reproductive process combines the sex cells of a male and female—doubling the chromosomes upon fertilization and bringing the total back to the normal number (in humans, 23 pairs, or 46).

Mathematically, the process of sexual reproduction (as opposed to asexual reproduction) allows more diversification. In humans, 3.2 billion base pairs of DNA in a man combine with 3.2 billion base pairs in a woman. (Evolutionists claim that the enormous potential variation in gene sequencing through sexual reproduction can lead to other forms of creatures, though they admit that such an idea is speculation.)[3]

Though different species may have the same *number* of chromosomes as humans, the DNA will be different. *It is the information encoded in the DNA that separates a human being from a spider* (also, the DNA strands will be observably different). The ability of DNA genes (sections of DNA) to generate protein products also differs greatly from species to species. All this raises an important issue confronting evolutionists: if species change from one to another, what mechanism changes—in fact, "improves"—the DNA?

DNA manages an amount of information beyond human comprehension, doing an incredible number of things in a tiny fraction of a second. It gives instructions to each part of the cell about such typical factory functions as:

1. generating power

2. manufacturing a great quantity and variety of products (proteins)

3. designating the function and relationship of these products

4. guiding key parts (molecules) to their final destination

5. packaging certain molecules in membrane-bound sacs

6. managing transfer of information

7. assuring a level of quality far beyond any human standard

8. disposal of waste

9. growth

10. reproduction

The makeup of the genes—that is, the grouping of the sections —of the DNA strand allows for 30,000 to 70,000 variations according to current estimates. There are also more complexity and more "splicing" alternatives than were once thought to exist. Hence, the available DNA information on the "production floors" (the *ribosomes*) is immense.

RNA is the substance that carries out the instructions of DNA. It is nearly the same as DNA, having six basic ingredients (more on this later). The easiest way to think of RNA is as a "reverse copy" of DNA that travels from the nucleus (the "computer center," where the DNA is) to the "production floor," where instructions for manufacturing a vast array of proteins are carried out.

The nucleus is like the "computer control room." It is where DNA is located and where the information is transferred from DNA to RNA. Within the nucleus occasionally there are found round structures called *nucleoli*. They surround sections of specific chromosomes and are believed to facilitate the production of *ribosomes*.

Ribosomes are essentially the "production floors"—where RNA instructions are received and various types of protein are "manufactured" depending on the RNA code. For instance, a human body requires literally thousands of different proteins to perform many tasks, from many needs within the cell to different types of protein to build hair, fingernails, muscles, and so on. In a single cell there may be many ribosomes, all producing vast numbers of different proteins.

Mitochondria are sites of energy production from cell respiration. A cell may contain hundreds of these sausage-shaped structures to provide all its energy needs.

Lysosomes process and rid the cell of destructive waste products. Essentially, they digest waste materials and food within the cell, using digestive enzymes (a protein produced within the cell) to break foods down into base elements.

The endoplasmic reticulum is like a transportation network for molecules within the *cytoplasm* (liquid substance of the cell). It transports the molecules to specific final destinations.

The Golgi apparatus is a form of "packaging center." It takes certain molecules and packages them into sacs, which are targeted to various locations within the cell "factory" or are even distributed outside.

Enzymes and regulatory proteins are produced by the cell for use in its own operation. Enzymes dramatically speed up certain activities of the cell. Some regulatory proteins (such as *polymerase*) in a sense turn genes "on" or "off"—permitting or preventing RNA replication depending on the needs of the cell. Many other regulatory functions are also accomplished by certain proteins, such as the built-in "proofreading" system. Without it, a cell might have a DNA copy error rate of 1 in 10,000. However, thanks to the error control system, copy errors *(point mutations)* range only from 1 in 1 billion to 1 in 1 hundred billion.[4]

The Cytoskeleton is the amazing "scaffolding" inside the cell. A far cry from normal factory walls, it can change and adapt in many ways, based on DNA instructions. For example, one key role is the holding of the *organelles* (the "organs" of the cell) in place. But the cytoskeleton must also be able to move to accommodate growth and reproduction. Many types of proteins in the cytoskeleton enable this.

Atomic and Subatomic Structure

So far we've looked at only the tip of the complexity of molecular biology—just a small portion of the cell and its substructure. Consider further the vast complexity of an organism like a human being. There are as many as 100 trillion cells in the human body performing thousands of specific functions. Each cell contains about a trillion atoms.[5] Therefore, we know the following:

- The human body contains 10^{28} atoms. That's more than all the stars in the universe.

- Further, as we noted in chapter 2, isotope studies indicate that 90 percent of our atoms are replaced annually.

- Every five years, *100 percent* of our atoms are replaced.

- In the last hour, 1 trillion trillion of your atoms have been replaced.[6]

The sheer numbers of parts and changes and the amount of specialization seem almost incredible. But scientists have learned about even more incredible instantaneous changes in our bodies at the subatomic level. For instance, a subatomic particle called the *xi* was found that has a life span of only one ten-billionth of a second. This means that, in only a few seconds, billions of xi particles have expended their life spans. Essentially, our body is changing at a rate close to the speed of light.

The "Mystery of the Cell"

Dr. Richard Swenson has brought together research by well-known scientists that gives even more evidence of the intricacy of the cell. He notes, "The mystery of the cell is both stunning and inspiring":

- Each cell is unimaginably complex. Each must live in community with its surrounding neighbors, doing its own specialized part in the whole.

- Each cell is surrounded by a membrane thinner than a spider's web that must function precisely, or the cell will die.

- Each cell generates its own electric field, which at times is larger than the electric field near a high-voltage power line.[7]

- Each cell contains specialized energy factories that synthesize *adenosine triphosphate* (ATP), which is the body's main energy source at the cellular level. Every cell contains hundreds of these factories, called *ATP motors*, embedded in the surfaces of the mitochondria. Each motor is 200,000 times smaller than a pinhead. At the center of each ATP motor is a tiny wheel that turns at about a hundred revolutions per second and produces three ATP molecules per rotation.[8]

- Cells don't stockpile ATP. Instead, they make it as needed from food consumed. Active people can produce their body weight in ATP every day.[9]

- Each cell has its own internal clock, switching on and off in cycles from 2 to 26 hours, never varying.[10]

Dr. Swenson goes on to say, "If after glimpsing the activity, intricacy, balance, and precision of life at this level you do not suspect a

God [or intelligent designer] standing behind it all, then my best diagnostic guess is that you are in a metaphysical coma."[11]

Swenson's comment urges us to really think. How likely is it that such vast complexity and precision could have come about by chance? Those who support naturalistic evolution have a real problem here. The problem is to explain how such intricate cellular machines, far beyond what humans could design, could randomly come together. What mechanism could have caused it? What is the mathematical probability that it could have happened in the time frame of a 4.6-billion-year-old earth? Or even a 15-billion-year-old universe?

The obvious problems include the following:

1. How would any individual component "know" when to arrive?

2. How would all the components randomly "know" how to assemble properly?

3. How would the cytoskeleton—the amazing protective "shell"—"know" to cover the cell to allow it to work?

4. How would all this complexity happen at once? (For instance, just having a mitochondrion by itself would do nothing—without DNA, RNA, and protein.)

5. How would a mitochondrion with its numerous minute ATP motors—each producing 300 ATP molecules per second—come about?

6. Where would the information for cells to work individually or as a system come from in the first place?

7. Lastly, the same question we've encountered before: What would initially energize life?

The DNA-to-Protein Process

Let's not make things any easier for those who are constructing the bridge of evolution. Let's go beyond what we've already examined about cellular operation in this chapter and take a closer look at the development of proteins from DNA. In essence, any plant or organism's cells are directed by preprogrammed instructions contained in its DNA. DNA's role is central.

Structure of DNA and RNA
How Protein Is Produced

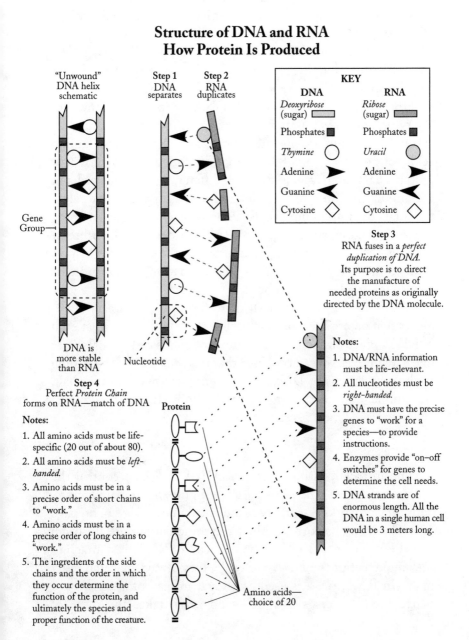

"Unwound" DNA helix schematic

Step 1 DNA separates

Step 2 RNA duplicates

KEY

	DNA		RNA
Deoxyribose (sugar)	▭	*Ribose* (sugar)	▭
Phosphates	■	Phosphates	■
Thymine	○	*Uracil*	●
Adenine	▶	Adenine	▶
Guanine	◀	Guanine	◀
Cytosine	◇	Cytosine	◇

Gene Group

Step 3
RNA fuses in a *perfect duplication of DNA.*
Its purpose is to direct the manufacture of needed proteins as originally directed by the DNA molecule.

DNA is more stable than RNA

Nucleotide

Step 4
Perfect *Protein Chain* forms on RNA—match of DNA

Protein

Notes:

1. All amino acids must be life-specific (20 out of about 80).

2. All amino acids must be *left-handed.*

3. Amino acids must be in a precise order of short chains to "work."

4. Amino acids must be in a precise order of long chains to "work."

5. The ingredients of the side chains and the order in which they occur determine the function of the protein, and ultimately the species and proper function of the creature.

Notes:

1. DNA/RNA information must be life-relevant.

2. All nucleotides must be *right-handed.*

3. DNA must have the precise genes to "work" for a species—to provide instructions.

4. Enzymes provide "on–off" switches" for genes to determine the cell needs.

5. DNA strands are of enormous length. All the DNA in a single human cell would be 3 meters long.

Amino acids— choice of 20

126 DISMANTLING EVOLUTION

Structure

If we were to unravel a DNA helix, we would see a ladder-type structure with phosphates and sugars on each vertical column. The "rungs" that attach to the sugar–phosphate sides are combinations of the bases: *thymine* (T) and *adenine* (A), or *guanine* (G) and *cytosine* (C). Those paired combinations are always TA, AT or GC, CG. No other combinations exist. The diagram on the previous page illustrates the structure of an unraveled DNA molecule.

From its six basic components, DNA can produce many necessary proteins. Each protein chain is made up of a few hundred amino acids, from among the 20 kinds of "life-relevant" amino acids (out of more than 80 amino acids found on earth).[12] Any protein chain can have many of each different kind, so the order of the amino acids in a protein determines its function. The selection of 1) the right amino acids, along with 2) the right grouping of amino acid clusters, and 3) the right order are all extremely important. None can be random in order for the protein to perform a function. The bottom line is, the formation of the proteins needed is complex and precise.

The proteins in any multicelled life-form are the primary ingredients that determine what each cell is structurally, and what each cell does. Since our bodies—and those of plants and animals—are made up of cells, we can conclude that it is protein, built according to the instructions of DNA, that determines what becomes hair, skin, bone, and all the organs of the body. It also determines whether we will be a plant, a human, or a toad.

Processes

The instructions built into the DNA molecule control the process of "telling" the ribosomes what proteins to manufacture. This process works essentially as indicated in the diagram on page 125. The DNA helix splits. Since the combinations are always in pairs (TA, AT or GC, CG), when "pieces" of RNA then attach to the single half of the DNA molecule, they always make an exact map. (In RNA, *ribose* is used as a sugar instead of *deoxyribose*— hence the "R" versus the "D"—and *uracil* takes the place of thymine.) The completed RNA molecule splits away and moves to the ribosome, where a protein is produced according to instructions carried by the RNA from the DNA. The DNA "knows" what the cell or organism needs next.

How? DNA is divided into groups of base-pair rungs we call *genes*. There are estimated to be somewhere between 30,000 and 100,000 genes on a DNA strand, and each gene "knows" how to make one type of protein. Therefore a DNA strand produces up to 100,000 proteins.[13] The genes direct all the traits of an individual, the order in which growth occurs, and feedback systems when repair or alterations are necessary.

Take, for example, the sequence of events from human conception, when a sperm and egg unite, through the process of differentiation. This is an issue no biologist understands. Yes, some facts are known. For instance, we know that, 30 hours after conception, the very first DNA molecule "commands" the very first cell division. The resulting cells each divide roughly twice per day. Since growth is exponential (each cell doubles twice a day), it doesn't take long for a couple billion cells to form. But what baffles scientists— especially evolutionists—is the stage when cells start to differentiate into arms, legs, toenails, retinas, and all the other parts of the body.[14] It's as if the DNA molecule is a highly designed supercomputer that knows exactly what to do, and when.

functions

So what does all the microdesign in that single DNA molecule result in? The average human adult's body—every *second* of every day—is organizing about 150 quintillion (150 x 10^{18}) amino acids into carefully constructed chains.[15] What do these chains of proteins do? They carry out a vast array of bodily functions, most of which the average person never thinks about:

- In a lifetime, a heart beats 2.5 billion times, never stopping to rest.

- In a lifetime, 60 million gallons of blood are pumped through your body.

- A red blood cell runs around your body 200,000 times over 120 days, only to be destroyed in the spleen on the 200,001st trip.

- Your body has grown 60,000 miles of blood vessels—the equivalent of two-and-a-half times around the earth.

- The number of red blood cells in your body, if laid end to end, would circle the earth four times.

- Billions of white blood cells die every time you get a fever, so that you may live.

- You breathe about 23,000 times each day, and the quantity of air you breathe weighs about 22 pounds.

- The small air sacs in your lungs (the *alveoli*), if cut apart and laid flat, would cover half a tennis court.

- The lung cilia that sweep mucus up the trachea vibrate at a rate of about 1000 times per minute.

- The eye is so intricate and complex that there is only one chance in 10^{78} that any two humans would have the same characteristics.

- In the retina there are 120 million *rods* (for dim, night, and peripheral vision) and about 7 million *cones* (for color and detail vision).[16]

- It would take a minimum of 100 years of Cray Supercomputer time to simulate what takes place in your eye every second.[17]

- The eye can distinguish millions of shades of color.

- The ear has a million moving parts.

- In addition to its complex hearing system, the ear has more than a hundred thousand motion-detecting hair cells that allow us to maintain balance and motion.

- Your nose can determine 10,000 different smells.

- Your body has 450 "touch" cells per square inch.

- There are estimated to be 100 billion neurons in the brain.

- Each neuron is estimated to have 10,000 branching fibers connecting it with other neurons.

- The brain has the capacity to store the amount of information contained in 25 million books (8 million more than are now in the Library of Congress).

- The brain makes about a thousand trillion computations per second.[18]

All of the above—and much, much more—just from one tiny DNA molecule that somehow "knew" exactly how to build and what to do for a particular person. Your body is vastly more complex than all the manufacturing facilities in the entire world put together.

———————

The idea that the body's vast microbiological complexity could have evolved from a simple bacterium exceeds belief. Where did all the information come from?

The more we learn about molecular biology, from the complexity of cellular structure to the vast complexity of our own human bodies, the more obvious it is that the bridge of evolution is not just swaying—it is buckling and crumbling.

Ten

Chirality: There's No Solution in Sight

In the previous chapter we looked at the development of a human being from the information in a single tiny DNA molecule. But what about the very first organism of life? Certainly it was far simpler than a human being. Are there any major obstacles for the theory of the random origin of the very first cell of life?

Most evolutionists believe that the very first cell of life was a simple bacterium. Current bacteria cells have about 128 million base pairs of DNA.[1] However, scientists have found ancient fossils of bacteria with only 500,000 base pairs. Some speculate further that it may have been possible for the earliest bacterium to have survived with as little as 100,000 base pairs of DNA.

Likewise, in the very first simple bacterium, there was a minimum limit to the number of amino acids for protein production. The accepted number is 10,000 amino acids with at least 100 functional protein chains—each holding a few hundred amino acids. Why are these numbers so important? Because of chirality.

What Is Chirality?

Chirality is the term given to the necessity that all nucleotides in a DNA or RNA chain be of a certain molecular orientation ("right-handed," technically *dextroform*) for the chain to work. The *nucleotides* are the "rungs" of the DNA ladder, composed of four ingredients, as we saw in the previous chapter. Again, *every single one* must be right-handed.

Likewise, nearly all of the 20 different amino acids used in cellular protein chains must also be of a specified orientation ("left-handed," technically *levoform*) for a protein to work. Not one can be defective. If these chirality requirements are not met, the entire process of manufacture from DNA to RNA to "working protein" fails. Hence, for the first bacterium, a perfect mix of both nucleotide orientation (right-handed) and amino-acid orientation (left-handed) had to occur. Even if we consider the simplest bacterium, we also need to keep in mind that both the DNA and protein chains are extremely long.

The Problem Presented by Chirality

In nature, however, we find that all amino acids occur randomly, in equal proportions of right- and left-handed (a *racemic mixture*). After years of study, scientists have not found a single means of *purifying* the mixture—that is, increasing substantially the proportion of left-handed amino acids. (The same problem, though more complex to explain, exists for nucleotides, which must be right-handed.) To create the first cell, *all of the thousands of amino acids in the hundred-plus functional proteins required for the first cell would have to suddenly show up—the right types at exactly the right place at exactly the right time—all left-handed.* This is the only way they would have been able to properly bond as instructed by the DNA.

Likewise, all 100,000-plus nucleotides would have to show up at exactly the right time in exactly the right way—all right-handed—to form a functioning DNA molecule.

In other words, to just get the 100,000 correctly oriented nucleotides together in the first place would be like flipping a coin and getting 100,000 heads in a row. To get the 10,000 correctly oriented amino acids together would be like flipping 10,000 tails in a row. To do both, which is necessary, would be like correctly getting 110,000 specified flips in a row.

Scientists Recognize the Problem

Some scientists have proposed ways around the chirality problem. Christian de Duve, of the Institute of Cellular Pathology in Brussels, Belgium, proposed a certain form of molecular modeling. Yet he went on to say,

> The proposed explanation does not entirely solve the chirality problem.

Later he says,

> Molecular modeling could not possibly help clarify this issue.[3]

Others have attempted to prove that chirality is not necessary and have failed. Dr. Alan Schwartz of the Evolutionary Biology Research Group at the University of Nijmegen in the Netherlands describes such an attempt:

> In an experiment designed to test the requirement for chiral purity, it was demonstrated that incorporation of even a single mononucleotide of opposite chirality into the end of a growing chain in template-directed oligomerization is sufficient to terminate the reaction (Joyce et al., 1984).[4]

Esteemed evolutionists clearly recognize chirality as a major problem.

A Mathematical Comparison

As we indicated earlier, randomly getting the correctly oriented compounds for the very first, simplest organism would be like correctly predicting 110,000 coin flips in a row. The probability of each flip being correct is of course 1 out of 2. One bad flip and the game is over. A direct calculation would simply be multiplying $1/2$ x $1/2$ 110,000 times. What are the odds that result? Very straightforward: $1/2$ ^{110,000}. Converted to base-ten, the odds are a staggering 1 in $10^{33,113}$!

This number is so large, it's like the chance of winning more than *4700* state lotteries in a row with a single ticket for each! Or, if we counted all the subatomic particles in the entire universe (10^{84})—in fact, in nearly 400 universes—it would be the same as the odds of selecting a single, predesignated particle from that number. Is it understandable why chirality alone is such a stumbling block for evolutionary science?

The Struggle with the Issue of Chirality

Notice what is being said about the problem of chirality by evolutionists:

> A recent world conference on "The Origin of Homo-chirality and Life" made it clear that the origin of this handedness is a complete mystery to evolutionists.[5]

The Web site of the University of California at Davis observes,

> Obviously, the origin of chirality is linked with the origin of life as we know it, so that same sorts of problems arise....There are several theories for the origin of chirality, none of them obviously superior to the others.[6]

Since no scientist can refute the mathematical impossibility of a random solution to the chirality problem, attention has been given to a means of *optically purifying* the particles (sorting them by orientation) and grouping the correct sorted particles together. This is where theories start to appear that suggest purification in outer space with some kind of transfer to earth. But such unsupported notions bring up their own problems, such as, where and how do the molecules get together? Can they really be purified

100 percent? How are they transported to earth? And, most important, where is the evidence?

At this point, unfortunately, some thinking begins to depart the scientific realm entirely. For instance, one Web site goes to great lengths in its attempt to give rational reasons for the random origin of DNA. But then the author stumbles:

> This [chirality] was discovered as long ago as 1848 by Louis Pasteur, and modern science calls it *biological homochirality.*
> Science has no explanation for this.[7]

This becomes such a problem for the author's theories that he later muses,

> What could cause a pre-organic engineer [alien] to create organic life using only half of the available amino acids? Why would he restrict himself to creating designs that were limited in this way?
> One possibility is that local conditions were such that only organic molecules of a particular handedness were available.
> ...If the first cell was created off-world, then this place is our best guess to start looking.[8]

In seriousness, this sort of thing is what even such esteemed theorists such as John Maynard Smith and Eors Szathmary are considering, as I noted in chapter 1.

Other suggestions have also been made, as an article in *Science* magazine reported:

> Origin of life researchers are attempting to look for weak forces that might explain how life consists of left-handed amino acids and right-handed sugars. Some of the "classic" mechanisms, such as circularly-polarized light from supernovae and other explosive astronomical events, have now been eliminated.
> Researchers have shown that such [circularly-polarized] light can skew chemical reactions toward producing one particular chiral molecule at the

expense of its twin. But supernovae and other astronomical sources would generate both the left- and right-spinning forms equally and so would be unlikely to produce an imbalance in organic molecules.

Even these problems ignore the more fundamental problem of high radiation levels that would be produced by these astronomical sources that are incompatible with living organisms or even complex organic chemicals.[9]

Scientists have struggled with chirality for more than a century. The problem is essential to our understanding of the origin of life. And, at least from the evolutionary viewpoint, no satisfactory answer has been found.

Therefore, it didn't surprise me that, when I researched evolutionary texts, chirality was strangely missing. Richard Dawkins didn't mention it, John Maynard Smith and Eors Szathmary didn't mention it, Mahlon Hoagland and Bert Dodson didn't mention it, Michael Denton didn't mention it, Edward O. Wilson didn't mention it, and only two of the twenty authors in André Brack's *Molecular Origins of Life* mentioned it. And it was extremely difficult to find an evolutionist Web site that could provide a reasonable discussion. If evolution were fact—and since chirality would be critical to the development of the first cell—shouldn't we have some answers?

———————

No matter how you look at it, the bridge of evolution seems to be on its way down. However, the existence of chirality and the statistical improbability that life began randomly seem to point to an intelligent designer—an engineer who carefully planned a strong bridge. But perhaps the most compelling evidence for a designer is what we noted earlier, in chapter 4—even if all the parts could somehow come together correctly, they would still need "someone to wind the watch."

Eleven

The Probability of the Random Origin of the first Living Cell

The previous chapters build a strong case for the beginning of first life being virtually impossible without extensive, purposeful design. This chapter will go even further and consider some other problems for the naturalistic origin of the first organism.

Experts Speak Out

Here's what some experts in the field are saying about the probability of the random origin of the very first cell:

- Marcel Schutzenberger of the University of Paris declared, "There is no chance ($<10^{-1000}$) to see this mechanism appear spontaneously; and if it did, even less for it to remain."[1]

- Molecular biologist Harold Morowitz calculated that, if every chemical bond were broken in the simplest living cell, the odds of it reassembling under ideal conditions would be $10^{-100,000,000,000}$.

○ Astrophysicist Edward Argyle states that a simple E. coli bacterium, with an information content of about 6 million bits, would have required about $10^{1,800,000}$ cases, or "states," to occur on the early earth for its inception to occur.[3]

○ John Horgan stated in a *Scientific American* article, "Some scientists have argued that, given enough time, even apparently miraculous events become possible—such as the emergence of a single-cell organism from random couplings of chemicals. Sir Frederick Hoyle, the British astronomer, has said such an occurrence is about as likely as the assemblage of a 747 by a tornado whirling through a junkyard. Most researchers agree with Hoyle on this point."[4]

○ The odds that all the functional proteins necessary for life might form in just one place by random events (not including all the other problems such as chirality) were calculated by Hoyle and his associate Chandra Wickramasinghe to be 1 chance in $10^{40,000}$.[5]

○ Thomas Huxley, an ardent supporter and contemporary of Darwin, once supposedly stated that six monkeys typing randomly for millions of years could type out all the books in the British Museum. David Foster, a cyberneticist, concluded that "Huxley was hopelessly wrong in stating that six monkeys allowed enormous time would randomly type all the books in the British Museum when in fact they could only type half a line of one book if they typed for the duration of the universe."[6]

○ Hoyle and Wickramasinghe provided calculations for a slightly different version of the Huxley claim—that instead of all the books in the British Museum, monkeys could type out the complete works of William Shakespeare. Their calculations indicated that the world was not large enough to hold the hordes of monkeys and typewriters (let alone the wastebaskets) required for such a feat. They indicated this was analogous to the unlikelihood of the random creation of living material.[7]

○ Gerald Schroeder continues the monkey analogy by stating that the chance of their randomly typing out any sentence at all, only a few words in length, is on the order of 1 in 10^{120}. He goes on to say, "Randomness just doesn't cut it when it comes to generating meaningful order out of chaos. Direction is required. Always." The odds with a world of monkeys and typewriters and a universe of time pale in comparison to the odds of just the chirality problem. And the problem becomes far greater when other factors are considered.[8]

○ Noted atheists Carl Sagan and Francis Crick were attempting to build a case for extraterrestrials (to gain research funding in that field). In the process, they estimated the difficulty of evolving a human by chance alone as $10^{-2,000,000,000}$. This would be in the same range as the estimate of Harold Morowitz.[9]

○ Stephen C. Meyer, who holds a PhD in the history and philosophy of science from Cambridge University, states, "While many outside origin-of-life biology may still invoke 'chance' as a causal explanation for the origin of biological information, *few serious researchers still do*."[10]

Some Factors and Their Probability

Here is a listing of some of the critical factors—a few of which we've already touched on—that are causing hard scientists, such as those above, to discard the notion of the naturalistic origin of the first cell.

1. Out of the 80 or so on earth, the *correct amino acids* must be selected. Only 20 are viable for life. Introducing any of the others could actually destroy life.

2. The *specific amino acid* needed by the protein chain must be added.

3. The *right amino acids* must be placed on the *correct portion of the chain* in order for the protein molecule to function.

4. On the DNA molecule, the *correct genes* must be formed.

5. The *sequencing of the genes* must be correct to properly instruct the organism.

6. There must be a *protective barrier around the genetic and protein* substance.

7. The *conditions of the environment* under which the organism is assembled must be acceptable for life development.

8. There must be a *viable source of energy.*

9. There must be *adequate time* for events to happen.

Let's take a look at the probabilities of some of these factors. We already know from examining chirality (see chapter 10) that the probability of naturally generating the correct orientation of the nucleotides and amino acids for the living cell is essentially zero (1 chance in 10^{33},[113]). What are some of the other major problems?

Getting only life-specific amino acids in the right place at the right time. As we've noted, only 20 of the 80 amino acids on earth are life-specific. For the very first cell, we need about 10,000 amino acids, and each has 1 chance in 4 of being correct (that is, $^{20}/_{80}$).

The calculation is virtually identical to the calculation for chirality—$^1/_4 \times ^1/_4$ for 10,000 iterations. Not unexpectedly, we get another highly improbable result:

$$1 \text{ chance in } 10^{6021}$$

But we're not done yet.

Each amino acid must be the right one. Since there are 20 life-specific amino acids, now we have a 1 in 20 chance to obtain the correct one—10,000 times. (Is it making sense why the enormousness of the mathematical problem is causing the most brilliant empirical scientists to completely reject naturalistic evolution as the cause of the origin of life?)

Let's continue with the math. Proper selection, as with the other two examples, means multiplication. This time, $1/20$ x $1/20$ again, 10,000 times. The result?

$$1 \text{ chance in } 10^{13,010}$$

...of getting the correct amino acids. And this probability goes on top of the others.

But there's more. We've only been dealing with the necessary amino acids. We haven't talked about the nucleotide side yet.

The proper material for each gene must come together so that each gene is capable of carrying out certain functions. In human beings, more than 3000 base pairs of DNA make up each gene, on average. However, we're dealing with the simplest bacterium. Its genes would not need to be nearly as sophisticated as a human's.

Taking the 100,000 base pairs we have been assuming—as the minimum scientists believe could support life—and taking the minimum number of genes of the smallest bacterium known (M. genitalium, which has an estimated 265 to 350 critical genes)[11] would mean that 377 base pairs would be required per gene. Each base pair has one of four choices: TA, AT, GC, or CG (see chapter 9). What are the odds of getting the right mix for one gene? Mathematically, it's handled the same as before: $1/4$ x $1/4$, for 377 iterations. For a single gene, the result is:

$$1 \text{ chance in } 10^{227}$$

However, we have estimated that 265 genes need to be correct. Although oversimplified, the point is still made when we calculate the magnitude of the need for all 265 genes to be correct. The combined probability would be the above result multiplied by 265:

$$1 \text{ chance in } 10^{60,155}$$

For DNA to properly direct the cell, the sequencing of genes must be correct. Now that we've selected the correct 265 genes, let's calculate the odds of the genes randomly being sequenced properly. For the first one to be right, the odds are 1 in 265. For the second to be right the odds are 1 in 264 (265 - 1). The odds of all of them being right are obtained by the multiplication of all the individual odds together. (Mathematically, this is called a *factorial function.*) Upon calculation, our result is

about 1 chance in 10^{528}

Compared to the other problems, this seems almost trivial. It's like winning only 75 lotteries in a row with a single ticket for each.

Final calculations. Now we add together all of our results. The probability of the naturalistic origin of the most simple bacterium we can conceive of, using only the factors we've discussed above, is as follows:

Factor	*Probability*
Chirality	$1/10^{33,113}$
Life-specific amino acids in the right place	$1/10^{6021}$
Correct specific amino acids in the right place	$1/10^{13,010}$
Correct material in the right place for each gene	$1/10^{60,155}$
Correct sequencing of genes	$1/10^{528}$
Total odds for the naturalistic origin of the most simple conceivable bacterium (conservatively figured)	$\mathbf{10^{112,827}}$

This would be like winning 16,119 state lotteries in a row with the purchase of one ticket for each.

Or it would be like picking a single predesignated electron out of more than 1300 universes as large as ours, assuming all matter was broken into subatomic particles.

The Problem of Time

Let's look at the problem a different way. '
estimate made by molecular biologist Harold Morowitz
chemical bonds in the simplest life-form were broken, the chance
of randomly putting them back together correctly is 1 in
$10^{100,000,000,000}$.

Let's take the entire universe and break it down into its smallest particles (we'll use baryons for our example). Scientists agree there are on the order of 10^{84} baryon-sized particles in the total universe. Then let's take all the time since the beginning of the universe, which most scientists believe is about 10^{17} seconds (about 15 billion years). Finally, let's assume that any one of these subatomic particles could interact with any other at any given moment (unlikely, since many would be light-years from others). Let's make one more generous assumption—that the maximum rate of interaction (rebonding) between particles per second is 10^{20}. (Although this rate is unknown, this very conservative estimate allows us to provide perspective on the problem of time.) What are the odds that the right chemical bonds could be re-established? Here are the factors:

Total number of possible interactions = 10^{84} x 10^{17} x 10^{20} = 10^{121}

Total interactions necessary to build the first cell = $10^{100,000,000,000}$

Probability of the naturalistic assembly of first life =

$$\frac{10^{121}}{10^{100,000,000,000}} = 0$$

In other words, the constraint of time shows us again that it is literally impossible to get the right stuff in the right place at the same time to form even the simplest of cells.

Other Challenges for Origin-of-Life Theories

If all the foregoing isn't enough to bring the bridge of evolution crashing down, we don't have far to go to turn up some additional

᷿les for evolutionary theorists. Interestingly, two of these ᴧigmas involve a couple of the most basic substances on earth.

Oxygen. Our lives depend upon the presence of this simple gas. Ironically, though, oxygen is a major problem for proponents of a naturalistic formation of life. The reason is, it destroys the building blocks necessary for life. (Of course, once a living cell is put together and protected, it's necessary for life.) To solve this problem, some scientists, such as Oparin, Haldane, and Urey, proposed an early-earth atmosphere with essentially no oxygen.

However, this creates a problem too. Oxygen—in the form of ozone—makes up a critical protective barrier against ultraviolet radiation in the upper atmosphere.[12] As molecular biologist Michael Denton points out,

> What we have then is a sort of "Catch 22" situation. If we have oxygen we have no organic compounds, but if we don't, we have none either.[13]

(Incidentally, recent scientific study indicates there *was* significant oxygen on the early earth.)

Water. A solution proposed to the oxygen problem was that the building blocks of life simply came together in the primordial ocean. If the first life-forms originated near underwater volcanic vents, they would have avoided the presence of oxygen gas.

There is a key problem with this idea too. According to evolutionary theory, DNA and protein molecules would have been built by adding one "block" at a time to an ever-lengthening chain. However, with the addition of each amino acid to a protein chain, or nucleotide to a DNA chain, a molecule of water is released. This is referred to as a *condensation reaction*.

A condensation reaction is essentially fully reversible. In other words, though

one amino acid + a second amino acid = protein + H_2O,

the reaction could also proceed in the reverse direction and decompose the protein:

protein + H_2O = amino acid + amino acid.

The same is true for DNA development:

$$nucleotide + nucleotide = DNA + H_2O$$

Or in reverse, the DNA is broken down:

$$DNA + H_2O = nucleotide + nucleotide$$

Why does this reversibility matter? As even first-year chemistry students are taught, a chemical reaction will *never* proceed in a direction that produces a compound already present in greater amounts in the reaction "vessel"—which is, in this case, water.

Therefore, to construct DNA and protein chains underwater from the amino-acid building blocks of life would be impossible.[14]

Information. Among the biggest dilemmas for supporters of naturalistic evolution is how information is programmed into the DNA structure to begin with. Where does it come from? How does DNA know when to start creating an arm or leg or ear? How does it know it's supposed to be a human, elephant, or fish?

These questions about systems apply also to the very first life-form. How did the DNA of the very first bacterium "know" how to program proteins to provide for its needs? How did it even "know" what its needs were? These things remain largely mysterious.

Do any logical solutions exist for these "catch-22" situations? We've methodically inspected the crumbling bridge of evolution, but all along we've also gathered some specifications for a different theoretical bridge. The components of the intelligent-design bridge suggest that

- fully formed organisms were placed in environments that were already suited for them

- a designer programmed the necessary information into life's components, just like a computer-software programmer puts information into software

As we go on, we'll accumulate more and more evidence that strengthens the intelligent-design structure.

Twelve

Mutations: A Faulty Mechanism

Okay. Let's try to hide all the evidence from molecular biology and mathematical probability analysis. Let's pretend we can get out the construction crew and rebuild the fallen bridge of evolution.

First, let's do an artist's rendering of a new bridge, one that ignores the obvious—that life was created. Let's simplify the design and do away with thousands of nuts and bolts and weld points, as if the cells of life were not so complex. Let's bring out the concrete trucks to pour the foundations for the piers, pretending that chirality really doesn't exist. Let's drive in cranes to raise the girders, assuming that amino acids don't really have to be so perfect for proteins to work. Let's restring the suspension cables, presuming we can always get the right components to make genes work and that their sequencing will always be perfect.

In short, we now have the skeleton of a new bridge that presupposes the naturalistic evolution of life. After all, we don't want to miss throwing in all the "fun stuff": dinosaur bones, old skulls, "monkeys to men," and especially mutations.

The Claim

The touchstone of evolutionary theory is the claim that mutations in DNA will eventually lead to improved species. To put it in perspective: First, a simple 100,000-base-pair bacterium mutated into slightly more advanced organisms. Exponentially, over time each organism then mutated into more and more organisms, until we arrived at the more than 1.7 million species we see today. (Actually, the rate of development would have to be much higher because species have been going extinct all along—presently, at an estimated rate of three species per hour).[1]

Virtually all biology and science textbooks base evolution upon mutation. For example:

> Biology textbooks are liable to say that mutations—that is, new heritable variants—are random....Can it really be true that mutations...led to the evolution of the wonderfully adapted organisms we see around us? This book [*The Origins of Life* by Maynard Smith and Szathmary] is an attempt to answer that question.[2]

> Scientists realize that mutations—changes in genes—are what produce new genetic characteristics (as well as inherited diseases). They further realize that without mutations, there can be no evolution.[3]

> Although mutation is the ultimate source of all genetic variation, it is a relatively rare event.[4]

> Beneficial mutations—if they are germinal [take place in the sex cells]—are the basis of evolution.[5]

All the above quotes indicate the assumption that favorable mutations as they are passed on, can lead to vastly different species. We'll look at this assumption from several perspectives.

What Is a Mutation?

A mutation is a random change in the nucleotides of a DNA molecule. It occurs during reproduction, when the DNA is being doubled in preparation for cell division (*mitosis*—see page 37).

Several things can cause a mutation. First there are random copying errors. These are extremely rare because DNA actually has its own "proofreading" system. Second, there are external effects, like radiation, that can cause a DNA molecule to mutate.

For mutations to be passed on to offspring, they must occur in the sex *(germ)* cells. Otherwise the mutation exists solely within the individual organism itself. However, it's rare that mutations spread through an entire population unless there is significant inbreeding. This is because in sexually reproducing populations, an organism's characteristics are made up from both the male and female parent. Therefore, the odds are 50 percent or less that a mutated gene will be passed on.

Virtually all mutations are harmful. They tend to create problems rather than provide an advantage. (More on the statistics of this later.) Populations with heavy inbreeding—therefore, more preserved mutations—tend to have more defects and more frequent health problems.

The sources referred to above all recognize the harmful effect of mutations:

> In general, new mutations are more likely to be harmful to survival than adaptive.[6]

> The altered information [mutation] shows up in the offspring, usually as a defect.[7]

> Mutations that give rise to substantial changes in the physical characteristics of the organism, however, are unlikely to be advantageous.[8]

> Most mutations that cause a visible change are harmful.[9]

Evolutionists, though recognizing that most mutations are harmful, still embrace them as the mechanism for evolution. Why? As mentioned above, mutations are the only hope for change from one species to another.

Real Change Between Species?

As noted in the last section, recent data shows that about three species are becoming extinct every hour. There is good evidence that the rate of extinction has rapidly increased lately, but extinction does raise a question: If mutational change is so effective in creating new species, why is there evidence throughout the past that we are losing some but gaining none?

Some evolutionists do point to what they call new species. However, it seems clear that those populations have simply experienced microevolutionary changes. An environmental impact has led to a change in the gene pool, and a visible change has resulted. This is the case with the peppered moth (see pages 68–70) and the polar bear (see later in this chapter), both of which have been cited as examples of new species.

Noted astronomer Fred Hoyle agrees with this conclusion:

> My impression is that some evolutionists have sought to speed things up by wrongly considering cases where species are only coping with environmental conditions they experienced before, so that memory is being misinterpreted as discovery.[10]

Hoyle goes on to cite the peppered moth as an example of the way many evolutionists misinterpret adaptation as development of a new species. After extensively using differential equations to evaluate the potential of positive mutations to develop new and different species, he concludes,

> Rarer advantageous mutations are swamped by more frequent deleterious mutations. The best that natural selection can do, subject to a specified environment, is to hold the deleterious mutations in check. When the environment is not fixed there is a slow genetic erosion, however, which natural selection cannot prevent.[11]

Changes Within Species

Before we delve into whether DNA mutations can actually make a change between species, let's look at an easier issue: mutations *within* existing species. As far back as the mid-1830s, the concept of natural selection was being discussed. For instance, the naturalist Edward Blyth (1810–1873), a contemporary of Darwin, reasoned that, if species could evolve to a greater extent through genera, families, orders, and classes, then why couldn't they evolve to a lesser extent when their environmental boundaries are threatened?

Blyth's reasoning was natural, but the facts are that when a species has a significant environmental change, its tendency is not to adapt, but instead to become extinct.[12] This supports Hoyle's observation of the failure of positive mutational change to outweigh negative mutational change. So does the fact that extinctions outpace the supposed development of new species.

Other mathematicians have also analyzed the effect of mutations. One of the world's great experts on the mathematics of evolution, Sir Ronald Fisher (1890–1962), who was also an architect of neo-Darwinian theory (and one of the founders of the field of population genetics), made one of the first mathematical studies on how natural selection works. Essentially he looked at offspring in populations, noting which offspring had a positive survival value (SV) because of a positive mutation or a negative SV because of a negative mutation. After considerable analysis, he concluded that

> most mutants, even if they have positive survival values, will be wiped out by random effects.
>
> ...A single mutation, even if it is a positive one, has only a small chance of survival. As a result, a single mutation is unlikely to play much of a role in evolution.

He summed up,

> If positive mutations are to play a role in evolution, many of them must occur.[13]

It's important to keep in mind that these observations came from an architect of neo-Darwinism.

Fisher's calculations, checked and recalculated by Dr. Lee Spetner, indicate that evolutionists are wrong to conclude that only a small number of positive mutational changes will take over a population. *The number must be massive.* And at this point we're talking only about *improving* a population, not about turning a lizard into a bird.

Mutations Are Like Typing Mistakes

One of the easiest ways to understand why mutations are almost always negative is to look at them like typing mistakes. Essentially that's exactly what they are: errors in conveying information. When a DNA molecule is copied and an error is made, that would be like typing a message and suddenly hitting the wrong key. What are the odds it will make an improvement? The following is a simple example:

The fox runs wild	The fom runs wild
The foa runs wild	The fon runs wild
The fob runs wild	The foo runs wild
The foc runs wild	The fop runs wild
The fod runs wild	The foq runs wild
The foe runs wild	The for runs wild
The fof runs wild	The fos runs wild
The fog runs wild	The fot runs wild
The foh runs wild	The fou runs wild
The foi runs wild	The fov runs wild
The foj runs wild	The fow runs wild
The fok runs wild	The foy runs wild
The fol runs wild	The foz runs wild

It's difficult to improve a sentence with a mistake, isn't it? The same is true of DNA, which is pre-programmed for a specific purpose. A mistake *takes away* information.

Mutations Don't Add Information

Assuming that mutation is the mechanism for evolutionary change, then mutations must be able to add information in order to develop more sophisticated organisms. If the first organisms were single-celled, with perhaps only 100,000 base pairs of DNA, and now we have humans, who are vastly more complex, with 3.2 billion base pairs of DNA, information had to be added somehow over time. As has been said, "Without mutation, there could be no evolution." Put another way, if mutations can't add information, there can be no evolution.

> But so far as known, or at least so far as I know, there are no such examples [of mutations adding information].[14]

In this statement, Dr. Lee Spetner is not claiming that there aren't mutations that help a creature survive. But he does indicate that these mutations simply change the function of a gene—they don't add anything.

Examples of Information Loss

All point mutations that have been studied have shown that not only is no information gained, information is *lost*. Let's evaluate some individual cases:

- *Bacteria resistant to streptomycin.* Some bacteria have built up a resistance to the antibiotic streptomycin through mutation. Normally, a molecule of the drug attaches to a matching site on a bacterium's ribosome, thereby interfering with its ability to make necessary protein. (Mammals don't have the same site on their ribosomes, so the drug doesn't hurt them.)

  The bacterium's mutation changes the shape of the site so the drug can't attach any longer. This mutation adds survival value to the bacterium and is inheritable, but it doesn't add any information. In addition, the loss of specificity (information) in the ribosome degrades the general performance of the bacterium.[15]

- *DDT-resistant insects.* Likewise, some insects have developed mutations that allow a resistance to DDT. DDT works by attaching poisonous molecules to matching sites on the insect's nerve-cell membranes. The mutations spoil the match, making the poison ineffective. Again, no new information is added; there is only a change. However, the cost of surviving DDT is losing specificity in the protein of the nerve cells.[16]

- *Polar bears' resistance to cold.* The polar bear has adapted superbly to its frigid environment. However, the mutations for adaptation lessen its survivability should the environment change.

- *Grains and vegetables with increased yields.* The yields of many edible plants have been increased through changes in the regulatory genes. Though the cells make more food protein, the cost is a loss of specificity in the plant's regulatory protein. Again, no new information is added.[17]

- *Dairy cattle with increased production.* Cattle bred for greater milk production turn out to be less fertile. Again, there is an overall loss of information.[18]

A 20-year series of experiments by evolutionary researchers originally suggested that cultures of bacteria could actually add information, thus forming a possible basis for macroevolution. However, evaluating the experiments in detail,

> We see that no new information got into the genome. Indeed, it turns out that each of those mutations actually lost information. They made the gene less specific. Therefore, none of them can play the role of the small steps that are supposed to lead to macroevolution.[19]

Summarizing our initial point, if mutations don't add information, and if addition of information is necessary for evolutionary development to occur, then macroevolution cannot occur.

A Statistical Analysis of the Probability of Mutations Leading to Macro Change

Dr. Lee Spetner, who holds a PhD in physics from MIT, has analyzed the likelihood of development of new species through mutation.[20] He selected horses for his analysis because they are very often used as examples of evolution.

Now, in order to calculate the odds of mutation creating a new species, we need to know

1. what the chance is of getting a mutation

2. what fraction of the mutations have a selective advantage

3. how many replications there are in each step of the chain of selection

4. how many of those steps there have to be to achieve a new species

What Is the Chance of Getting a Mutation?

Considerable research has been done on the chance of obtaining a mutation. Studies indicate that the probability of a mutation varies according to the species. For example, bacteria have the most mutations, with a rate of between .1 and 10 per billion transcriptions. (To return to our typing example, this would equate to one error in 50 million pages of typing—the lifetime output of about 100 professional keyboarders.) However, other organisms have a mutation rate of 1 in 10 billion (10^{-10}).[21] So we'll use a mutation rate of 10^{-10}.

What Fraction of Mutations Have an Advantage?

In order to cause a selective advantage that can lead forward to a new species, a mutation must have two components:

- It must have a positive selective value ("help" the species).

- It must add a little information to the genome.

As we have already seen, this second point is a problem. We have no evidence whatsoever that mutations have added information to the genome of an organism. However, for sake of this analysis, let's assume it's possible and continue.

The first point also presents a problem. How many mutations must happen to have a positive selective value adequate to improve a given population? Sir Ronald Fisher admits it would take "many," as we noted earlier. A minimum mutation would be that of one nucleotide, and some biologists (for example, Richard Dawkins) assume that even the most minimal mutation can trigger macroevolutionary change. At this point, let's assume we don't know how many mutations would be required to get an adequate selection value for a macro change so we can continue with the analysis.

How Many Replications Are Necessary to Make a New Species?

The smaller the change in each step, the more steps are needed. Another architect of neo-Darwinism, the late G. Ledyard Stebbins, estimated that it would take about 500 steps to create a new species.[22] The question then becomes, how many births would be required for a small evolutionary step to occur? Paleontologists who have studied horses over their theorized 65-million-year development have provided information to Dr. Spetner that leads him to conclude it would take about 50 million births.

Returning to the Problem of Advantageous Mutations

Moving back to the previous question we didn't answer: What fraction of mutations must be advantageous (adaptive) in order to create a selective advantage? No one really knows, except that, as Fisher pointed out, there would have to be many. So in order to continue, let's turn the question around and see how many advantageous mutations it would take to cause evolution to "work." This way, we can judge whether or not the number is actually realistic.

We need to start by giving a "value" to the "typical" mutation. This value indicates the contribution the mutation makes to favorable species change. The late George Gaylord, generally acknowledged as the "dean of evolutionists," indicated a "frequent value" is about a tenth of a percent.[23] Spetner uses that in his calculations.

Survival of Mutations

"Next," says Spetner, "We move to evolutionist and population genetics expert Fisher's calculations that for only *one* mutation with a tenth of a percent selective value, the odds are 500 to one against its survival.…There would have to be 1100 of them to have a 90% chance of survival."[24]

Here we begin to see the problem with mutations causing one of the steps assumed to be necessary for the evolution of horses. First, the positive mutation has to occur (with an adequate selective value), then it has to survive, then it has to take over the population. The chance that such a mutation will appear in the population is 1 in 600 ($1/600$). If it has as high a selective value as one-tenth of a percent, the chance that it will survive is 1 in 500 ($1/500$). Thus, the chances of it appearing, surviving, and taking over the population would be $1/600$ x $1/500$ = $1/300,000$.

But there's a further statistical problem for evolutionists when we use their own numbers in our calculations. The above 1 chance in 300,000 is simply for *one* step of the *500* said to be necessary to effect an evolutionary change. In order to calculate what it would take for all 500 steps to take place, assuming no errors, we would have to multiply $1/300,000$ by itself 500 times. Our result is $2.7/10^{2739}$ This is a probability that a statistician would call impossible. It would be like winning 391 lotteries in a row with a single ticket for each one. And keep in mind the following:

- This is only one change in the evolutionary ladder.

- We used numbers supplied by evolutionists.

- We yielded on contentions that we believe to be false, such as the assertion that a mutation can add information.

When we place the evolutionary idea of mutation under critical analysis, we discover that there is no evidence of mutations adding information. Using numbers and assumptions from evolutionists to estimate the probability of mutation achieving only one improved species, we get an impossible result.

So we didn't get far with our reconstructed bridge. The mechanism of mutation turns out to be just as insubstantial as the other evolutionary contentions we have looked at previously.

Thirteen

Irreducible Complexity: A Major Transitional Problem

The boys' hearts were pounding in anticipation. They had just stumbled on an advertisement from a local dealership: "Beautiful, brand-new, red Corvette convertible. Top of the line, one of a kind. Only one available! First person to claim it tomorrow morning can have it for only $19,000! Cash only. No camping in our parking lot."

"You've got to be kidding!" exclaimed Luke. "I've always dreamed about one of these, but the cheapest I've ever seen one for is about fifty-five grand."

"I know," said Matt, "but how on earth can we have a chance of getting it?"

"Well, first, if we both took our money out of savings and pooled our cash, we probably could come up with the money to own it together."

"Yeah, but that place will be crawling with people," Matt moaned. "How could we have the chance of being first anyway?"

"I've got an idea," replied Luke. "My brother works at a mechanic's shop. We could just dress up in some mechanics' clothes and walk in like we're guys going to work and go right up to the front before the rest!"

"Brilliant!" Matt yelled. "Let's do it!"

The guys spent the day gathering the funds, finding the mechanics' suits, and talking excitedly about cruising around in a first-class automobile with the top down.

Finally morning arrived, but Luke and Matt had been up long before dawn. As expected, a large crowd had assembled outside the roped-off lot. The plan worked flawlessly. They passed the "rent-a-cop," fooling him completely—just like they were employees. When the time came to open the doors, they had strategically placed themselves at the front.

The doors opened, and the guys were nearly trampled by the throng of people behind them—but sure enough, they reached the target first.

"You boys ready to purchase this fine high-performance machine?" asked the salesman.

"You bet!" they blurted out excitedly.

"You got that much cash?" he queried, recognizing they were pretty young.

"Ye...ye...yessir!" they finally stammered.

"Okay then, no sense wasting any time—you can see we've got a lot of people behind you. Just sign these forms here and the car is yours."

As the guys signed the forms, the dejected crowd started to slowly disappear.

Finally, the car was theirs. After flipping a coin to see who got the driver's seat first, Luke won, and they both got in the bright red Corvette. For just a moment they sat in the plush leather seats, enjoying the smell of the new car, their minds racing about the fun they were about to have.

Then Luke reached down and turned the ignition key. Nothing happened. He turned it again—nothing! He honked the horn, and the salesman came running out. "Hey, what's your problem?" he barked.

"This car won't start," Luke said in frustration. "What's wrong?"

"Well—it needs an engine to run. But we sell 'em here and have several choices," the salesman rumbled. "I'd recommend our Excalibur V-8—it makes it run like a real firecracker. It'll run you about $50,000 installed."

The dream was turning into a nightmare.

"Oh, and by the way, you'll want to buy a drive train too. Ya need one, ya know," wheezed the salesman. "Again, we can help you select what's best for you. We've got one on the lot right now that will do the job. I can make a special deal for you—maybe $15,000."

That was it. The boys left in their old car, minds scrambled, not knowing what to do. Things aren't always the way they appear.

Irreducibly Complex Systems

The bright red Corvette needed all its parts in order to function at all. The beautiful exterior appearance did absolutely nothing. The same can be said in biology. From Darwin to Richard Dawkins, evolutionary claims have been made based on looking at just the exterior of organisms—the "macro" portions. They may look easily designed on the outside, but it's an entirely different story on the inside.

If we took just the car's engine, it alone could be broken down into hundreds of parts vital to the function of the car. The drive train likewise. But living systems, at the cellular level, are infinitely more complex than just a car body, an engine, and a drive train. Not only would we need to throw in the equivalent of gas tanks, spark plugs, engine seals, radiators, fuel lines, pistons, electronic ignition systems, fuel pumps, exhaust systems…we'd have to throw in a few trillion other parts as well—all put together in the right way at the same time. This makes many living systems *irreducibly complex.*

Michael Behe, well-known molecular biologist and author of the book *Darwin's Black Box,* and the champion of the concept of *irreducible complexity,* describes it this way.

What type of biological system could not be formed by "numerous, successive, slight modifications" [the premise of evolutionary theory]?

Well, for starters, a system that is irreducibly complex. By irreducibly complex I mean a single system composed of several well-matched, interacting parts that contribute to the basic function, wherein the removal of any one of the parts causes the system to effectively cease functioning.[1]

As with the car example above, if the proposed macroevolution of a system cannot happen *gradually*, and if the system is necessary to increase the survival value of a species, then the system could not have been brought about by evolutionary processes.

A Basic Illustration of Irreducible Complexity

Behe explains the basic premise of his model in terms of a simple mousetrap.

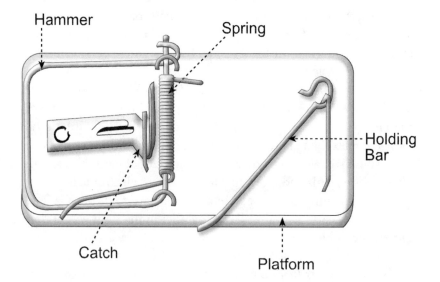

Hammer

Spring

Holding Bar

Catch

Platform

Notice that the components of the mousetrap include

1. platform
2. hammer
3. spring
4. catch
5. holding bar

If we put the mousetrap into the context of gradualistic evolution, we might imagine the platform evolving and remaining in a population. However, it by itself has no survival value, so in all likelihood it would disappear. It certainly wouldn't catch any mice. Likewise, the hammer might evolve within a population for a while, but again, since it has no survival value by itself, it also would probably disappear from the population. The same could be said for each one of the components of the mousetrap. In order for any one part to have any mouse-catching value, *all the parts must be available at one single time*—not to mention the necessary information and the energy to set the trap.

Yet, even this very basic illustration oversimplifies things. If the platform were not strong enough, it wouldn't work—it couldn't withstand the tension of the spring–hammer combination. If the spring were not strong enough, it wouldn't work—it couldn't project enough force to kill a mouse. If the catch were too short, it wouldn't reach the hammer...and so on.

Cellular Systems Are Much More Complex than a Mousetrap or Car

Consider a macro change involving a system of cells. The cellular system's complexity is vastly greater than all of the manufacturing facilities in the world put together. Think of just the ATP motors in mitochondria—let alone all the other functions cells need to perform—and the complexity of DNA instructions that we saw in chapter 9.

In Darwin's day, it may have been understandable to look at beak types in finches and, in the macro sense, assume that one finch had evolved from another. Even in the mid-twentieth century, it was perhaps justifiable to hold that apes and humans were related because of their appearance. Today, with molecular biology, it's not. With the electron microscope, X-ray crystallography, and nuclear magnetic resonance imaging, we can peer into the actual makeup of genes and the function of living cells.

Michael Behe makes a relevant observation. When, toward the beginning of the twentieth century, neo-Darwinian theory was being synthesized, there was one important group that was absent—the molecular biologists. Why? Because neither the discipline nor its tools existed! As in the example below, much of the criticism of irreducible complexity is made by biologists who haven't learned to "think small" enough yet.

The Premise regarding the human eye, as argued by Francis Hitching:

It is quite evident that if the slightest thing goes wrong en route—if the cornea is fuzzy, or the pupil fails to dilate, or the lens becomes opaque, or the focusing goes wrong—then a recognizable image is not formed. The eye either functions as a whole or not at all. So how did it come to evolve by slow, steady, infinitesimally small Darwinian improvements? Is it really plausible that thousands upon thousands of lucky chance mutations happened coincidentally so that the lens and the retina, which cannot work without each other, evolved in synchrony? What survival value can there be in an eye that doesn't see?[2]

A Response by zoologist Richard Dawkins to Hitching's argument:

[Hitching] also states, as though it were obvious, that the lens and the retina cannot work without each other. On what authority? Someone close to me has had a cataract operation in both eyes. She has no lenses in her eyes at all. Without glasses she couldn't even begin to play lawn tennis or aim a rifle. But she assures me that you are far better off with a lensless eye than with no eye at all. You can tell if you are about to walk into a wall or another person. If you were a wild creature, you could certainly use your lensless eye to detect the looming shape of a predator, and the direction from which it was approaching.[3]

Why is Dawkins' remark out of date? It's because of its implication that the eye could have evolved in partial macro steps (for instance, without a lens). It also implies that the remainder of the eye—the incredibly complex retina and its light-sensitive cells—is a whole and that it all could have developed at once. This old way of thinking can no longer be supported by the molecular biochemical evidence. If evolution is going to work, it must work at the cellular level or not at all.

Getting Down to the Real Analysis

In order to have macro value in a population, mutations need to be positive, they need to survive, and they need to have a high enough selective value—about .1 percent. (We analyzed this in chapter 12.) With a system as significant as the eye, we should be able to assume that the selective value would be high enough.

The problem would arise with the enormous number of mutations it would take to have all of the necessary sub-systems mutate at the same time. After all, with the human eye, we're considering more than just the easily seen parts—the cornea, the iris, the pupil. We also have to account for the lens, the muscles attached to the lens, the retina with its 120 million rods and 7 million cones, and many other parts, not to mention a brain that has to know how to process the information. Every one of these subsystems is made up of countless cells—each cell being a miniature "factory."

Let's consider the simplest, most basic part—the light-sensitive cell (a single rod or cone). We'll review it from a modern biochemical model. The following is a paraphrase of Michael Behe's description, found in his landmark book, *Darwin's Black Box*.[4]

The Biochemical Cycle of a Light-Sensitive Cell

1. Light strikes the cell, and a photon interacts with a molecule called *11-cis-retinal*.

2. This rearranges within picoseconds (the time it would take light to travel the width of a hair) to turn into *trans-retinal*.

3. The change in the shape of the retinal molecule forces a change in the shape of the protein *rhodopsin*, to which the retinal is tightly bound.

4. The protein's metamorphosis alters its behavior—it's now called *metarhodopsin II*.

5. The altered protein sticks to another protein called *transducin*.

6. Before bumping into metarhodopsin II, transducin had been tightly bound with a small molecule called *GDP*.

7. When the transducin interacts with metarhodopsin II, the GDP falls off, and a molecule called *GTP* binds to the transducin.

8. *GTP-transducin-metarhodopsin II* now binds to a protein called *phosphodiesterase*, located in the inner membrane of the cell.

9. When attached to the metarhodopsin II group, the phosphodiesterase acquires the chemical ability to "cut" molecules called *cGMP* in the cell. The phosphodiesterase lowers the concentration of cGMP, just as a pulled plug lowers the water level in a bathtub.

Another membrane protein that binds cGMP is called an *ion channel*. It acts as a gateway to regulate the number of sodium ions in the cell. Normally the ion channel allows sodium ions to flow into the cell, while a separate protein actively pumps them out again.

The dual action of the ion channel and the "pump" keeps the level of sodium ions in the cell within a narrow range.

---

10. When the concentration of cGMP is reduced because of cleavage by the phosphodiesterase, the ion channel closes, causing the cellular concentration of positively charged sodium ions to be reduced.

11. This causes a current to be transmitted down the optic nerve to the brain.

12. The result, when interpreted by the brain, is vision.

———————

If the reactions mentioned above were the only ones that operated in the cell, the supply of 11-cis-retinal, cGMP, and sodium ions would quickly be depleted. Something has to turn off the proteins that were turned on and restore the cell to its original state.

In the dark, the ion channel, in addition to sodium ions, also lets calcium ions into the cell. The calcium is pumped back out by a different protein so that a constant calcium concentration is maintained.

———————

13. When cGMP levels fall, shutting down the ion channel, the calcium ion concentration decreases too.

14. The phosphodiesterase enzymatic reaction, which destroys cGMP, slows down at a lower calcium concentration.

15. A protein called *guanylate cyclase* begins to resynthesize cGMP when calcium levels start to fall.

16. While all of this is going on, metarhodopsin II is chemically modified by an enzyme called *rhodopsin kinase*.

17. The modified rhodopsin then binds to a protein known as *arrestin*, which prevents the rhodopsin from activating more transducin. (Thus we see that the cell contains mechanisms to limit the amplification of the signal started by a single photon.)

18. Trans-retinal eventually falls off rhodopsin and must be reconverted to 11-cis-retinal. It must be re-bound to rhodopsin to get back to the starting point for another visual cycle.

19. To accomplish this, trans-retinal is first chemically modified by an enzyme to *trans-retinol*—a form containing two more hydrogen atoms.

20. A second enzyme then converts the molecule to *11-cis-retinol.*

21. Finally, a third enzyme removes the previously added hydrogen atoms to form 11-cis-retinal, and the cycle is complete.

All of this process takes only a few picoseconds—and it takes place in 127 million rods and cones in each eye.

Immediately, we observe that the process is far more complex than Darwin or any soft-science biologist ever dreamed of. It's hard enough to conceive of how evolution could assemble the overall structure of the rods and cones. But the real difficulty comes when we dig into the individual cells and analyze specifically what they do. Any single step of the 21 listed above would result in lack of vision. So the mutations that must occur to create a light sensitive spot can be generalized into four stages:

1. *Accumulation of the necessary base molecules* for the process in a single location in the first place

2. *Assembling the structural elements* in a mechanical system that will allow the chemical system to work

3. *Developing the complex process* outlined above that results in electronic impulses to the brain

4. *Teaching the brain* how to interpret such signals

The concept of irreducible complexity indicates that all of the above would have to happen simultaneously because any partial light-sensitive spot would have absolutely no survival value. If it had no survival value, the mutation(s) would die out.

Facing the Data

How realistic is it that mutations would actually randomly produce such a light-sensitive spot in a population? We might argue that the necessary base molecules could be assembled in a single location randomly.

But the minute we move to stage 2, the problem becomes substantially greater. Now we are asking the mutations to add considerable information—how to structure something simultaneously with all the other things that must come together at once.

The problem is taken to a further extreme once we move to stage 3. Now enormous amounts of mutational information are necessary (just review the complexity of the system's 21 steps listed above). At this point we need the molecules, the correct structure, and a highly complex chemical system to all have mutated at exactly the same time. Then the final straw is the necessity of the brain's sudden realization of how to use this new neural input.

In reality, 140 million such light-sensitive cells had to come together in each eye. But for the eye to work, many other parts are needed, each with its own microbiological irreducible complexities: the optic nerve, the contents of the eyeball, the lens, the cornea, the muscles, and so on. And if all of these individual irreducibly complex parts can't come together at once through simultaneous mutations, the survival value of the eye is worthless. Again, you can't catch many mice with just a block of wood.

Blood Clotting: Another Amazing System

The clotting of our blood is something we all take for granted. If we get a small cut or abrasion, we expect the blood to quickly form a clot that prevents both further loss of blood and infection. Seldom do we consider the complexity of this system, which has to "know" exactly when and where to perform its function. It must clot wherever needed, even if a wound is a very deep one. On the other hand, it cannot form a clot too easily, or within the body, else it would destroy our heart and blood vessels.

When viewed at the biochemical level, the clotting of blood is another irreducibly complex system. So complex is it that Michael Behe takes 33 pages in *Darwin's Black Box* to explain it.[5]

When confronted with such systems, experts in naturalistic evolution sometimes fail to address the details and the hard, probabilistic facts. For instance, an esteemed biochemist from Harvard's Center for Molecular Genetics, Russell Doolittle, reviewed then-current knowledge of the mammalian blood-clotting system in the journal *Thrombosis and Haemostasis*.[6] His question was, how could such a complicated process arise?

Behe's analysis of the article indicates that Doolittle is painting a "step-by-step Darwinian scenario involving the undirected, random duplication and recombination of gene pieces."[7] The language used includes presuppositions of evolution—phrases like "is born," "springs forth," "is unleashed," and so forth. In sum, Behe calls Doolittle's overview of blood clotting

> seriously inadequate because no reasons are given for the appearance of the proteins, no attempt is made to calculate the probability of the proteins' appearance, and no attempt is made to estimate the new proteins' properties.[8]

Gene-Shuffling to Account for Blood Clotting

Suppose we address the issues that Doolittle seems to ignore in his article. How much "gene-shuffling" would be necessary to make a new blood-coagulation protein randomly?

In his calculations, Behe's opening assumption is that animals with blood-clotting *cascades* (a "trip-wire" sequence of reactions, each touched off by the reaction previous to it) have roughly 10,000 genes, each divided into an average of three pieces. As a result there would be 30,000 gene pieces that would have to be "shuffled." A necessary binding agent, TPA (tissue plaminogen activator), has four different types of "domains."[9] Therefore, through random shuffling, the odds of getting those four domains together is $30,000^4$. This would be about the same as 1 chance in 10^{18}—almost the same odds as those of winning three state lotteries in a row with a single ticket for each. (This isn't as impressively impossible as some of the other evolutionary scenarios in this book—however, I have yet to hear of someone who has won two consecutive state lotteries with one ticket for each, let alone three.)

Behe also points out that his calculation is extremely generous. After all, the domains would have to

- have the correct linear order
- be in the active area of the genome
- have in place the correct signals for splicing
- be compatible in their amino acid sequences

Logically, it doesn't seem possible that the necessarily immense number of highly complex, integrated mutations could possibly take place simultaneously in order to form entire sophisticated systems. Further, we have to keep in mind what we saw in the previous chapter:

- Positive mutations are very rare.
- Mutations generally don't survive in a population.
- Mutations don't add information.
- For the development of a complex system, a large number of simultaneous positive mutations would have to survive and take over a population.

As we see from both Dawkins and Doolittle, the necessity of irreducibly complex components has not been accounted for in biochemical models of naturalistic evolution. This is another question that has not been answered by neo-Darwinists. In summary, irreducible complexity seems to point us down the road again, toward the other bridge—the bridge of intelligent design.

fourteen

Nanotechnology: Engineers Copy Our Own Cellular Machines

Nanotechnology is one of the buzzwords of the twenty-first century.

By way of definition, "nano" has been used for decades as a prefix indicating a billionth (10^{-9}) part of something. So "nanotechnology" essentially deals with very small things—in terms of billionths of a meter. In many cases we are referring to the manipulation of actual atoms or molecules themselves—a world we now have access to through electron-microscope techniques, X-ray crystallography, and magnetic-resonance imaging.

We've already demonstrated, though, that the world is still very far away from the ultimate design in small machinery—that which is found in life itself. Consider just a few examples we've mentioned before:

- The miniature *ATP-production motors*, 200,000 times smaller than a pinhead, that are the energy factories for our bodies. Each has a tiny wheel at its center that turns at about a hundred revolutions per rotation, producing three ATP molecules per rotation. Every cell in our body has hundreds of these nonstop motors, adding up to literally hundreds of trillions in our bodies. [1]

- The *electrical field* of each cell, which at times is more powerful than the electrical field near a high-voltage line.[2]

- The *cellular clock* contained in each cell that cycles precisely over periods from two to twenty-six hours, never varying and never stopping.[3]

- *Lung cilia*, which sweep mucus up the trachea and vibrate at a rate of 1000 times a minute.[4]

- The *light sensitive spots* of the 7 million cones on the eye, each capable of distinguishing millions of shades of color.[5]

- The more than *120 million rods* on the retina that have a sensitivity to as little light as one or two photons.[6]

- *The human eye*, which is so complex that it would take a Cray Supercomputer more than a hundred years to simulate what a single eye does every second.[7]

- The more than 100,000 miniature *motion sensors in the ear,* which can maintain the balance of a human being weighing hundreds of pounds.[8]

- *The DNA molecule*, which can store information equivalent to that on five high-density computer disks—all within the space of a thousandth of a millimeter.

Machines, Not Organisms

The incredible design of the motors and systems in cells far surpasses anything human beings have ever been able to design themselves. Even some convinced evolutionists have abandoned language that seems to indicate that living cells are evolved "organisms."

For instance, evolutionist Michael Gross talks about the development of nanotechnology in his book *Travels to the Nanoworld*. When discussing how scientists are now very serious about investigating the natural technology designed into the cellular machines in our bodies, he uses the following terminology:

> Let us have a first look at these "natural nanomachines," to see whether they could serve as models for scientists and engineers trying to develop new technologies.[9]

Many evolutionists have stopped talking about "organisms"—and are using the more accurate term "machines." They think that, somehow, these systems still evolved, but their biomechanical aspects and potential benefits are being recognized—again, for instance, by Michael Gross:

> We are talking about complicated and highly efficient *machines* having a size of only a few millionths of a millimeter.[10]

Even the subtitle to Gross's book reads "Miniature Machinery in Nature and Technology." That's quite a difference. A machine performs work *for a purpose*—and is *designed*.

For Progress, Think Small

Dr. Gross goes on to support what we've already discovered about the structure of a cell:

> Nothing ever produced by human engineering efforts comes anywhere near the performance of these biological systems.
> [For instance,] biomolecules, which are found within every living cell,...can carry out the most amazing tasks.
> ...It will become clear that nature's superiority is much more obvious on the nanoscale than in large-scale engineering.[11]

Gross's final point emphasizes what we've already seen: that only from the smallest scale can we draw firm conclusions about the origin of life.

Overall, *Travels to the Nanoworld* indicates the boom in interest in nanotechnology and what we can gain by peering into cells, studying their machines, and modeling or duplicating them:

> [The rise in the use of the prefix "nano"] actually allows us to assess the progress that science has made toward the world of the invisibly small, the nanoworld.[12]

> We are investigating these systems…so that we can compare them with artificial nanoscale systems that have recently been created, and to find inspiration for even more powerful nanosystems that we are only beginning to dream of.[13]

Which Is It?

In the same breath, however, Gross is quick to maintain the evolutionary viewpoint. He states,

> The secret behind this success story, the underlying principle that has been proven the best (if not the only) way to efficiency on a small scale by *3 billion years of evolution*, is the modular *design principle*.[14]

Now wait a minute. That really hedges his bets. "Evolution" used in the same sentence as "design principles." Which one is it? Dr. Gross seems to agree that the amazing biosystems are designed. Yet he still begins, as do many other biologists, with a presumption that evolution is fact. He also maintains that

> at the beginning of life on Earth, the step from nothing at all to the first cell took much less time than the step from cells to multicellular organisms.[15]

Unfortunately, this pronouncement doesn't explain away all the problems. Gross provides no evidence—he simply makes a statement he assumes people will readily accept. He doesn't address the hard-science probabilistic issues of the naturalistic origin of life. Nor does it face up to all the evidence we've uncovered that supports intelligent-design theories.

We Are Now Using Molecular Biology to Learn Design

Suppose you wanted to learn how to play the guitar. Where would you go? Would you go find just anyone on the street? Of course not. Would you look for someone who played worse than you do? No. You would search out someone who played guitar better than you and who presumably was a good teacher as well.

Suppose you wanted to build a bridge to carry heavy trucks. If you'd never done it before, and especially if you were not an engineer, you would probably look for a model. Where would you look? Would you go to someone's beautifully landscaped garden and look at the decorative bridges? I doubt it. Would you go into an African jungle to copy a footbridge? It might get you started, but it probably wouldn't get you very far. Or would you try to find a model that already worked to carry heavy trucks?

Top scientists and engineers in the world are now looking at what *works*. They're digging into biochemistry for secrets to design. Yes, *design*—that is far beyond human capability. How serious is the twenty-first century about nanotechnology design? Well, apparently the United States government takes it *very* seriously.

The National Nanotechnology Initiative has set up special agencies to analyze and take advantage of what we're beginning to learn. Included in the governmental groups appointed to analyze nanotechnology are the following:[16]

- the Department of Agriculture
- the Department of Commerce
- the National Institute of Standards and Technology
- the Department of Defense

- the Department of Energy
- the Department of Justice
- the Central Intelligence Agency
- the Department of Transportation
- the Department of the Treasury
- the Department of State
- the Environmental Protection Agency
- the National Aeronautics and Space Administration
- the National Institutes of Health
- the National Regulatory Commission
- the National Science Foundation

Clearly, the U.S. government takes the design that is exhibited in life systems extremely seriously and is investigating its application.

Paley's Watch

William Paley, in his 1802 book *Natural Theology*, used the example of a watch as an argument for the existence of God. If someone were walking through a field and saw a stone, he suggested, they would never stop to ask how it got there. On the other hand, if a person noticed a watch lying in that field, a number of questions might arise. The observer would stop, would probably pick it up—but certainly anyone would recognize it as something designed, not randomly developed, even if they had never seen a watch before.

As we noted in chapter 4, a watch would obviously be recognized as a designed object. But a watch is almost infinitely more simple than an average cell, which is one-thousandth the size of the period at the end of this sentence. Molecular biologists recognize this. Michael Gross recognizes this, although he apparently dosen't analyze what it would really take to randomly assemble life.

Other evolutionary scientists have also failed to address this issue. For instance, author and zoologist Richard Dawkins refers to Paley's watch story in the name of his popular book *The Blind Watchmaker*. In the book, Dawkins pokes fun at Paley's example. He uses no hard empirical analysis to support his claims, but he simply indicates that evolution is a well-known fact.

Isn't it more reasonable to follow the lead of top scientists from 15 agencies of the U.S. government—the ones who have chosen to call cellular systems *designed,* and who want to apply this design to nanotechnology? Science is now going in the reverse direction of naturalistic evolution, as it were. Instead of simply presuming that a "blind watchmaker"—chance—will turn humans and other organisms into new and improved species, researchers are now using molecular biology to investigate the machinery of life and figure out the design that's already there. Their objective is to study how these micro machines work so that we might approximate them.

What Researchers Hope to Achieve Through Nanotechnology

Nanotechnological advances may eventually be made by constructing things a molecule at a time, or even an atom at a time. Observing the machinery of the cells has stimulated much thought and creativity. Here are some examples of what's being predicted.

Manufacturing. Self-replicating machinery might eventually be produced at a molecular level, as in the human body. Since there is a practical limit to the current methodology used to reduce the size of computer chips, this could greatly affect computer technology. If we can learn to replicate systems the way the body does, the manufacturing possibilities are virtually endless. For example, Zyvex, a nanotechnology company, points out,

> Manufactured products are made from atoms. The properties of those products depend on how those atoms are arranged. If we rearrange the atoms in coal we can make diamond. If we rearrange the atoms in

sand (and add a few other trace elements) we can make computer chips. If we rearrange the atoms in dirt, water and air we can make potatoes.[17]

Medicine. Since biosystems are being analyzed down to within the cells themselves, medical applications are virtually endless. Some of the applications being considered are—

- *Cancer-killing artificial cells.* "The device would have a small computer, several binding sites to determine the concentration of specific molecules, and a supply of some poison which could be selectively released and [would be] able to kill a cell identified as cancerous."[18]

- *Artificial red blood cells.* "Poor blood flow, caused by a variety of conditions, can result in serious tissue damage. A major cause of tissue damage is inadequate oxygen. A simple method of improving the levels of available oxygen despite reduced blood flow would be to provide an 'artificial red blood cell.'"[19]

- *Artificial mitochondria.* The vast complexity of the mitochondria has already been mentioned. Can we really duplicate these complex machines? "While providing oxygen to healthy tissue should maintain metabolism, tissues already suffering from ischemic injury [tissue injury caused by loss of blood flow] might no longer be able to properly metabolize oxygen. In particular, the mitochondria will, at some point, fail….However, more direct metabolic support could be provided…Devices restoring metabolite levels, injected into the body, should be able to operate autonomously for many hours."[20]

Handling of energy. "There are solid engineering predictions that nanomachines should be able to convert between mechanical, chemical, and electrical energy with almost 100% efficiency and extremely high power density. Power storage will become far easier and more reliable, allowing the use of solar energy for virtually all energy needs."[21]

Computer technology. "Computers will be more powerful by a factor of about 1,000,000,000. We can't predict what they will be used for; who could have predicted desktop computers and the World Wide Web back in 1950? But human-class artificial intelligence becomes a lot easier when your desktop computer has the raw power to simulate every neuron in a human brain."[22]

Space travel. "Aerospace advances due to improved materials and manufacturing will allow spaceships to be about as common as cars are today. We could literally lift the entire population of the earth into space, with minimal environmental impact and low financial cost."[23]

Environmental implications. "Nanotechnology will allow us to build almost anything we can imagine today out of almost pure carbon, with no industrial waste. If you don't want something anymore, just burn it—someone else will pull the CO_2 out of the air and make something useful with it."[24]

Naturally, all these projections about the future are something like the ideas on the 1960s cartoon show *The Jetsons*. And not many of those have come true today. Obviously, a lot will depend on our ability to duplicate, however remotely, the design that already exists in cellular systems. (Incidentally, to my knowledge, those who are making such predictions are not predicting a new species of humans—just longer and healthier life for the present variety of humans, thanks to biomechanics.)

———————

Isn't it interesting that top scientists now speak of the *design* of cells? Isn't it telling that systems and subsystems of cells and organisms are now referred to as *machines?* Even people who simply assume that evolution must be fact—regardless of statistical evidence—now use these terms.

Yet designs simply don't happen by random chance. Machines aren't built by "blind watchmakers."

Where is naturalistic evolution amid all this amazing design?

Fifteen

Intelligent Design and Information Theory

Ideally, science operates on the basis of free inquiry. Multiple hypotheses compete for validity, and the one with the best evidence is considered the most viable. However, since Darwin's time, free inquiry has increasingly been replaced with a presumption of naturalism, especially among those supporting evolution. Here's the way naturalism views the world:

> The universe (nature) is the only reality. It is eternal, self-activating, self-existent, self-contained, self-dependent, self-operating and self-explanatory. The universe is not derived from nor dependent on any supernatural or transcendent being or entities.
>
> All phenomena can be explained in terms of inherent interrelationships of natural events without recourse to any supranatural or supernatural explanations. No reality exists other than processes in space and time. There are no nonnatural causes.[1]

A Limiting Paradigm

The problem we face with naturalism is not with the fact that it is one of a choice of worldviews. Rather, the difficulty is that scientists who embrace naturalism to the exclusion of all other worldviews take away the basis of free inquiry. In other words, once we limit ourselves to a specific paradigm, such as naturalism, we limit the questions we might ask or the research we might conduct.

As an example, take a court case. Imagine that the suspect in a murder had left fingerprints on the murder weapon, had left drops of blood at the scene that matched his DNA, and had been seen committing the murder by an eyewitness. Then suppose that, through legal technicalities, the defense was able to get all three of these pieces of evidence thrown out so the jury would never hear them. The effect of this would be to severely limit the questions that could be asked and increase the likelihood of a conclusion not in accord with reality. The murderer might well be set free.

The same is true of a presumption of naturalistic evolution. By limiting the questions, the answers can be effectively "guaranteed." In many cases, evolutionists are very straightforward about doing this. For instance, the *American Journal of Physical Anthropology* recommends to its readers,

> In any confrontation, you should be prepared to show that evolution is scientific, not that it is correct....One need not discuss fossils, intermediate forms, or probabilities or mutation. These are incidental. The question is, what is science, and what is religion?
>
> Therefore, if you must confront the creationist, we suggest you discuss the nature of science, the kind of knowledge it can provide and the kind it cannot provide.[2]

How incredible! First there is the indication that being correct is not an issue. Second, there is the implication that evidence is "incidental." This is hardly scientific.

The naturalistic presupposition is very common despite overwhelming evidence of design. One example is the following statement:

> Biology is the study of *complicated* things that give the
> appearance of being *designed* for a *purpose*.[3]

Here we can see the zoologist Richard Dawkins recognizing that
1) biological systems are complex, 2) they have the appearance of
design, and 3) the design is apparently for a purpose. It is only the
assumption of naturalism that prevents him from saying, "What
looks like a duck, acts like a duck, sounds like a duck, and smells
like a duck, must *be* a duck."

Francis Crick (winner of the Nobel Prize in Physiology or
Medicine, 1962) also limits his capability for free inquiry by
holding a naturalistic worldview. He maintains,

> Biologists must constantly keep in mind that what they
> see is not designed, but rather evolved.[4]

These words were written even *before* all the vast advances in
molecular biology in the 1990s. We could wonder, if naturalistic
evolution is so obvious, then why do we need such constant
reminding that things are not designed?

Now, intelligent-design theory is challenging preconceived
notions that naturalism is the only way to view the world. New
questions are being asked. Free inquiry has brought forward *information theory* as a new basis on which to compare naturalistic evolution and intelligent design.

Introducing Design and Information Theory

How do we differentiate design and information from randomness? Let's consider the following set of letters:

ETH

To most people, these are simply three letters chosen at random
out of the 26 letters of the alphabet. They neither show design nor
constitute information. Other letters could just as well have been
chosen randomly, such as ZNK, ORS, MEQ, FHI, RCU...or
many other variations. None of them tell us much.

But suppose the letters were arranged like this:

T H E

Suddenly, we start to wonder if this new arrangement is by design. What changed? Simply the organization of the letters, not the letters themselves. Was information added specifically to create a pattern we recognize—the word "the"? Before we jump to accepting this pattern as a purposeful design, there are a few things that need to be considered.

1. The pattern of letters would only be recognizable as a word if we had a "receptor," so to speak—previous knowledge that there was such a word.

2. If we assume we were limited to the three letters T, H, and E, the odds of the word THE randomly occurring are quite high. After all, which choices do we have with those three letters? THE, TEH, HTE, HET, ETH, and EHT. Each has a probability of $^1/_6$—nearly 17 percent. The pattern THE could easily be considered random.

The Link Between Design and Information

Design and information are linked together. Design implies that information has been applied to accomplish a purpose. But at what point do we separate design from something that could occur by random chance or *constrained chance* (which we will define shortly)?

The answer is, *the point at which it becomes no longer statistically acceptable to account for the presence of information without some intelligent agent.* To determine this point, we need to evaluate the following two things:

1. the degree of *complexity*

2. the degree of *specificity*[5]

In the example above, the letter pattern ETH was neither complex nor specific. It was meaningless. Even when the arrangement was changed to THE, it gained only specificity. It still lacked complexity, as demonstrated by the relatively high probability that those three letters could simply have been randomly arranged that way.

At What Point Do We See Design?

In order to carry this example further, so we can see when a pattern starts to cross the boundary into becoming evidence of design, let's pretend we have several trays of Scrabble-type letters to work with. There will be 5 trays, containing, respectively, the sets of letters indicated below. The symbol "_" means a space, which has as much importance as a letter. Our purpose in analyzing the trays will be to determine the degree of complexity and specificity in the sets of letters, based on the number of them and the way they are arranged. We will then use our results to deduce which trays contain information which might lead us to the conclusion of intelligent design in the contents of the tray.

1. E T H

   - not complex
   - not specific

2. I R _ M _ S P L U E F _ E T E _ A T E D H E _ A O _ F I H F T _ E A G _ S _ E N C L E _ G T _ L D A N C T O _ I L _ E G A T O

   - complex
   - not specific (that is, meaningless)

3. T H E

   - not complex
   - specific

4. U N I T E D _ S T A T E S

   - very complex
   - very specific

5. I_PLEDGE_ALLEGIANCE_TO_THE_
   UNITED_STATES_OF_AMERICA

○   extremely complex

○   extremely specific

What conclusions can we draw from our example?

○   It is the *arrangement of components* that creates information. Notice that the letters in tray 2 and tray 5 are identical. Those in tray 2 are nonsensical—however, those in tray 5 are informative.

○   A *degree of complexity* is necessary before any mix of components can be construed to contain information or be designed. In tray 3, even though the letters THE make a word, the pattern would not be considered of sufficient complexity to bear the sign of information input by design.

○   When we get to the set of letters in tray 4, we could easily start to argue for design. The sequencing UNITED STATES contains 13 specific letters arranged in a special way that makes sense to those with knowledge of English.

      Is the sequencing *complex enough to constitute information* coming from design? Well, the probability of those letters randomly forming the words UNITED STATES is 1 chance in 6,227,020,800 (just over 1 in 6 billion). To put it in perspective, there is far more chance that you will be killed by lightning this year than that these letters would randomly organize themselves in this way.

○   In the last tray, tray 5, we find *extreme complexity and extreme specificity* that certainly *constitute information*. Even though some may consider this a small number of letters—62—the odds of their randomly forming this pattern are slightly over 1 in 10^{85}! (This would be like winning 12 state lotteries in a row with a single ticket for each.) This sequence of letters clearly shows evidence of intelligent design.

A "Filter" to Detect Design

Dr. William Dembski proposed a model for evaluating design versus nondesign in his book *The Design Inference: Eliminating Chance Through Small Probabilities*.[6] Essentially, his model takes an event through four decision classifications to determine whether it is designed or nondesigned. It "filters" the event by asking whether it can be explained by the phenomena listed below:

Dembski's Explanatory Filter

1. *Law*. For example, the law of gravity.

2. *Chance*. Pure, random chance.

3. *Constrained chance*. Random chance with a constraint that affects it.

4. *Design*. Purposeful design by an intelligent source.

The filter first asks the question, is this event explained by natural laws? For example, a rock falling to the ground needs no explanation other than the fact that gravity is a natural law that exists and pulled it to the ground.

If the event is not explained by a natural law, we move to the second category. Was the event caused by pure, random chance? A card selected out of a deck would be an example of a purely random event. No law would affect the selection (assuming there is no cheating). There is a 1 in 52 chance that any single card would be selected.

Then we go on to the third category. *Constrained* chance is still a chance event, but there is a constraint—a limiting or predisposing factor—that makes certain parts of the event more likely. An example of this would be gold miners panning or sluicing for gold. A quantity of sand believed to contain gold is placed into a pan and shaken. The selection of the sand would be random, as would the lateral movement of the materials. However, the constraint is the weight of the gold, which would cause it to settle to the bottom.

If none of the above categories explain an event, we could assume that it was caused by design.[7] Such is the case with the complexity of a watch (remember Paley?) or a violin.

Another Way to Deduce Design

Dembski's explanatory filter is represented differently in his later book *Intelligent Design: The Bridge Between Science and Theology*. In this version, he uses some terms that we've already discussed—*complex* and *specific*—as well as the term, *contingent*, which means "dependent on or conditional by something else" (Webster). Here's how the filter[8] operates:

1. Is the event *contingent?*   If NO =   Necessity

    If YES

    ↓

2. Is the event *complex?*   If NO =   Random

    If YES

    ↓

3. Is the event specific?   If NO =   Random

    If YES   →   =   Design

At step 1 the question is, is the event contingent? If not, then it is the result of a physical law, and the analysis stops. Continuing, the model would ask if the event is complex. If not, it is attributed to chance. If so, the line of questioning moves on to the quality of specificity. If the event is not specific, it again falls into the realm of randomness. But if it is specific as well as complex and contingent, it falls into the realm of design.

Comparing Naturalistic Evolution with Design

Using the above model, along with the facts presented in this book, we can reach some conclusions regarding the theories about the origin of today's species.

Phenomenon: Life

1. *Contingency:* Yes. A human amino-acid chain contains about 10,000 amino acids connected to a "spine" (similar to a charm bracelet). There is no specific "law" that governs this connection—it is programmed by the RNA, which is programmed by DNA instructions. It is contingent.

2. *Complexity:* Yes. As we've seen throughout this book, all cellular systems are incredibly complex—again, whether caused by naturalistic evolution or design.

   A now-familiar example is the structure of amino acids and the 3.2 billion base pairs of human DNA. A vast number of components must all be in correct order for the protein chains and DNA to work.

3. *Specificity:* Yes. Molecular biology, as we've noted repeatedly, reveals that the information provided by amino-acid and nucleotide chains is extremely specific.

   Then, chirality alone provides a degree of specificity that would preclude randomness. When we then look at gene sequencing, we find this to be the case even more.

Therefore, the degree of complexity and specificity in life favors a conclusion of design.

When the presupposition of naturalism is laid aside, we can deal with the evidence according to free inquiry. We can ask whatever questions we want. Under these conditions, an objective analysis shows that intelligent design better accounts for the facts than naturalistic evolution.

As an explanation for the origin and development of life, the bridge of evolution has crashed down. In contrast, the bridge of intelligent design looks strong enough to bear the weight of current facts and discoveries.

This will continue to be the case in the next chapters, as we go back to before the origin of life—to the beginning of the universe.

Part 5

The Macro: Moving from a Flawed Structure to a Firm One

Physics: How Do We Explain the Contradiction Between Two Natural Laws?

Webster defines "contradictory" things this way:

> Either of two propositions related in such a way that it is impossible for both to be true or both to be false.

Moving back in time from the origin of life, let's look at the beginning of the universe and consider the two alternative ideas about its origin:

1. The universe began naturalistically.

2. The universe was created by an intelligent designer.

Throughout this book we've been examining much evidence that bears on the conflict between these two contradictory points of view. What things from physics might lead us to either a conclusion of naturalistic evolution or intelligent design?

As it turns out, the divide between the two theories of origins is reflected in another contradiction. Based on the discoveries of the twentieth century, two of the fundamental laws and principles of physics now seem to be at odds with each other.

Let's take a look at this conflict and see if it can be resolved in a way that tells us something about where the universe came from. First, though, we'll need some background.

What Is Physics?

> Physics is the science that deals with such basic ideas as energy, force, matter and time. It explains how the world around us is put together and how it changes. Physics comes from the Greek word meaning *nature*.[1]

From this definition, we might expect the laws of physics to support the concept of naturalistic evolution. But before we jump to that conclusion, let's take a look at the historical development of physics and see how recent advances in physics have shaped our understanding and our ability to examine the question of the universe's origin.

Some Quick History Points in Physics

Engineering by trial and error was probably the earliest type of physics. For example, people learned how to use logs to roll heavy loads, or how to design and craft bows that could shoot arrows. Experimentation entered the scene later. For instance, about 200 B.C. Archimedes discovered that the weight of a floating body equals the weight of the water it displaces.

A mature system of mathematics was necessary for physics to come of age. Mathematics finally allowed great thinkers and engineers to abstract the phenomena we observe in nature, such as energy, force, matter, and time, and deal with them precisely and predictably.

Leonardo da Vinci, for instance, was associated with the beginning of modern physics. During the fifteenth and early sixteenth centuries, he studied mechanics and created designs using physics.

A Few Key Developments in Modern Physics

A key event of the start of modern physics took place in 1543, when Nicolaus Copernicus published his discovery that the earth and planets revolved around the sun. Centuries of key break-throughs then followed:

- 1600: William Gilbert initiated the study of electricity and magnetism.

- early 1600s: Galileo discovered key laws in many fields of physics.

- 1678: Christian Huygens formulated the wave theory of light.

- 1687: Sir Isaac Newton published his *Principia Mathematica,* in which he developed the basic laws of mechanics. (Incidently, Newton also invented calculus.)

- 1730: Daniel Bernoulli developed the kinetic theory of gases.

- 1798: Count Rumford (Benjamin Thompson) defined that the motion of particles in a substance creates heat.

- 1803: John Dalton proposed the atomic theory of matter.

- 1850: James Joule published experimental results showing that heat and energy are interchangeable at a fixed rate (a foundation of the first law of thermodynamics).

- 1873: James Clerk Maxwell published equations developing the electromagnetic theory of light.

- 1895: Wilhelm Roentgen discovered X-rays.

- 1897: Sir Joseph John Thomson discovered the electron.

- 1900: Max Planck established the foundations of quantum theory.

- 1905: Albert Einstein proposed special relativity.

- 1915: Einstein proposed general relativity.

- 1924: Edwin Hubble discovered galaxies beyond our own.

- 1926: Erwin Schroedinger published his development of the principles of wave mechanics.

- 1929: Hubble discovered redshifts in distant galaxies that indicated the expanson of galaxies and the universe.

- 1965: Arno Penzias and Robert Wilson confirmed 3° K. (Kelvin scale) background radiation as evidence of Einstein's general relativity theory in support of the big-bang theory of an expanding universe.

- 1992 on: The mapping of the edges of the universe was begun, using millions of data points provided by the COBE space explorer.

The above shows a rough approximation of the development of the hard science of physics, and provides dating of some of the key discoveries made by scientists mentioned later in this chapter.

Thermodynamics

> *Thermodynamics* [is the] field of physics that describes and correlates the physical properties of macroscopic systems of matter and energy. The principles of thermodynamics are of fundamental importance to all branches of science and engineering.[2]

There are four basic laws of thermodynamics. The *zeroth* and *third* laws are not relevant to our analysis. But the *first* law is important to our review of the apparent contradiction between two of the basic principles of physics. The *second* law is sometimes brought into discussions about evolution versus creation, so we'll mention it briefly before we go on to the first law.

The Second Law of Thermodynamics (Entropy)

Entropy defines how close a system is to equilibrium. One way to illustrate entropy is to think of a cube of sugar, a packet of powdered creamer, and a cup of hot coffee. Before they are mixed, they are in three different states of order. But when they're added together, gradually a state of disorder takes over until maximum disorder is reached and there is a state of equilibrium or maximum entropy.

> The law states that the entropy—that is, the disorder—of an isolated system can never decrease. Thus, when an isolated system achieves a configuration of maximum entropy, it can no longer undergo change: It has reached equilibrium.[3]

In other words, things always tend to go from a state of order to chaos, not the other way around, unless there is a purposeful input of energy. Things run down. Everything from our bodies to machines, buildings, and the universe itself is running down.

There is an important component to the second law of thermodynamics that is sometimes overlooked, though—that the law applies to *isolated systems.* When we look at the universe as a whole, it would indeed be considered such an isolated, or *closed,* system.

However, we must use caution when attempting to apply entropy to the proposed process of evolution of living things, because despite the apparently closed nature of the typical reproduction processes of organisms, it is not *entirely* closed. For example, radiation and other external factors can still change an outcome. Energy can accidentally or purposefully be added.

Nonetheless, the system is *essentially* closed, and the second law would seem to apply. We could wonder how a tiny organism like the proposed original bacterium *added* order and evolved into a highly complex human. But we shouldn't be too dogmatic on this point.

It's interesting to note one thing, though. Although knowledgeable physicists sometimes criticize creationists for forgetting that the second law requires a closed system, other physicists attempt to use it anyway to disprove the current big-bang model of the universe. (Why? As we will discover, the big bang actually supports the model of intelligent design.) For example, plasma

physicist Eric Lerner, author of *The Big Bang Never Happened,*
declares in this regard that

> the laws of nature cannot explain the amazing advance
> in complexity of living organisms that has taken place
> on Earth over the past 4 billion years.[4]

The second law is certainly true in relationship to the cosmos
as a whole. However, the issues we've presented in this book more
than adequately make the point that naturalistic evolution is statistically unreasonable. We don't need to complicate things by
trying to apply the second law to the theorized physical evolution
of living things.

The First Law of Thermodynamics

This is the law of *energy conservation.* The law states that the
total energy of a system plus its surroundings remains constant. It
also states that energy and matter can neither be created nor
destroyed, although matter can be converted to energy (such as
the burning of wood or the fission of radioactive materials) and
vice versa. The first law, like all the other laws of thermodynamics,
has been verified by repeated testing and experimentation, so there
is virtually no doubt about its accuracy.

The first law becomes especially important regarding the origin
of the universe. Why? Because we know that energy and matter
exist in the universe today. Where did they come from, if they can
neither be created nor destroyed?

For many years, especially when the laws of thermodynamics
were being formulated in the nineteenth century, scientists believed
the universe was infinite in duration. As late as the famous "Scopes
Monkey Trial" in 1925, there were still plenty of scientists who
held that the universe was infinite (or at least adequately old to
allow for evolution).

Certainly an infinite universe would answer the question of
where energy and matter came from (that is, it was just "always
there"). But is it accurate scientifically? Does it contradict some
other fundamental principle?

The Principles of Relativity

Special Relativity

In 1905, Albert Einstein published his now-famous theory of *special relativity*.[5] Its well-known equation is $E = mc^2$, or Energy = Mass times the speed of light squared. While experimental confirmation of this theory brought Einstein much acclaim, it is his theory of *general relativity* that is most applicable to the question of the origin of the universe.

General Relativity

In 1915, Einstein announced his theory of general relativity. General relativity builds on special relativity, adding in the influence of gravity and other factors defining the motion of the universe. It deals with how the universe should have originated and is highly testable by experimental physics.

Einstein noted, in 1916, that his field equations of general relativity predicted an expanding universe, a notion that was unacceptable to him at the time.[6] Why was this prediction of his own theory so objectionable? It was because it implied that there was a beginning to the universe, rather than that the universe was infinite, which was the commonly held scientific belief of the day. Einstein concluded that, if there was a beginning to the universe, there must have been a "beginner" or intelligent designer of the universe. At the time, he was not able to accept this conclusion.

He capitulated and added a "cosmological constant" in order to allow his equations to come back into agreement with the vogue of an eternally existing universe. In essence, his constant cancelled out the effects of gravity everywhere in the universe.[7] Later, when his friend Edwin Hubble and others experimentally demonstrated that the universe was in fact expanding, Einstein discarded the cosmological constant, eventually calling it one of his greatest blunders ever.[8]

Interestingly, in 1998 the journal *Science* gave "the discovery of the cosmological constant" the "Breakthrough of the Year" award (though the constant wasn't really proven until April 2000). However, this constant is quite different than the one Einstein had originally proposed, and actually strengthens the evidence for the big-bang model.[9]

The Big Bang and General Relativity

In the background information we've reviewed so far, we've seen two contradictory ideas about the universe: 1) It always existed; 2) It had a beginning. Let's take a closer look at the experimental model that supports the idea that the universe had a beginning—the big-bang model.

The "big bang" is a term that was coined at the time scientists were originally speculating on the origin of the universe based on the theory of general relativity. In a nutshell, Einstein's equations (along with the updates based on experimental physics) indicate that the universe started from nothing and burst into existence. Unfortunately, the term "big bang" makes it sound like a chaotic explosion. As we'll see in the next chapter, nothing could be further from the truth. Rather, the development of the universe has the appearance of unfolding an environment precisely tuned for mankind.

How Reliable Are General Relativity and the Big Bang?

Some of the key breakthroughs of twentieth-century physics involve phenomena that affect the study of the origin of the universe. Experimentation throughout this time has tended to support the big bang model. Here are some of those developments.

Hubble's Discoveries

In the 1920s a contemporary of Einstein, Edwin Hubble, documented that the most distant galaxies are moving away from the earth. Furthermore, the farther away the galaxies are, the faster they are receding. His experimental finding that showed this is termed the *redshift*.

To illustrate, consider the way we experience the Doppler effect with sound. With, for instance, an approaching train, the pitch of its noise is higher because the train is coming toward you, in effect compressing the wavelength of the sound waves reaching your ear. After the train passes by, however, the reverse happens—the sound wavelength expands, and the pitch decreases suddenly.

Likewise, the redshift of distant galaxies implies that they are moving away from us since red is the longest wavelength of visible light. The "degree of redness" indicates speed. Even though Hubble was the first to document an expanding universe, a great number of experiments have been done since to confirm *Hubble's law,* as it is termed.[10] For example,

> In 1996 two teams at the Carnegie Observatories engaged in measuring Hubble's constant by different methods reported converging findings on the age of the universe. One team, led by Wendy L. Freedman, estimated the age at 9–12 billion years. The other, led by Allan Sandage, estimated the age at 11–15 billion years.[11]

Background Radiation

In 1964 and 1965, Bell Labs' Arno Penzias and Robert Wilson were working with a large space antenna located in Holmdale, New Jersey. They noted a 3° K. "background" radiation that came literally from all directions of the universe. (Ironically, other scientists had observed the same background radiation before, but had simply dismissed it as an anomaly.)

About the same time, Princeton University's Robert Dicke, looking for additional evidence of the big bang, had postulated that if the big bang had occurred, a remnant of very low-level radiation would be resonating throughout the universe. Penzias and Wilson's discovery thus provided strong confirming evidence for the big bang. (In 1978, Penzias and Wilson were awarded the Nobel Prize in Physics.)

Mapping the Background Radiation

The COBE (*CO*smic *B*ackground *E*xplorer) space probe was launched in 1989 by a team under the leadership of George Smoot of the University of California at Berkeley. It was equipped with a great deal of sophisticated equipment, including instrumentation that could compare the spectrum of background radiation with that of a precise "blackbody." The probe was designed to confirm or deny the big bang as the origin event, and to map cosmic background radiation precisely.

On April 24, 1992, the news hit. The research team was heralded around the world for "discovering the edges of the universe." By then the COBE spacecraft had beamed back a tremendous number of data points confirming background radiation and mapping the universe.

Stephen Hawking, Cambridge University's Lucasian professor of mathematics, said, "It's the discovery of the century, if not of all time."[12] Michael Turner, astrophysicist at Fermilab and the University of Chicago, indicated that the discovery was "unbelievably important....The significance of this cannot be overstated. They have found the Holy Grail of cosmology."[13] Project leader Smoot exclaimed, "What we have found is evidence for the birth of the universe." He added, "It's like looking at God."[14]

Since 1992, there have been numerous independent experimental confirmations of results of the COBE breakthroughs. The data from other sophisticated information gathering tools has simply confirmed what Penzias and Wilson originally observed in 1965.

The Search for Helium

The big-bang model states that, by the time the universe was 20 seconds old, there would have been a high proportion of helium (estimated to be about 25 percent of all matter). One of the ways to examine the likelihood of the big bang is to determine the elements in existence in the universe at its very edges. These areas would have been the first to be formed, and if a high proportion of helium exists in them, this would support the big-bang model.[15]

In 1994, astronomers measured an abundance of helium in very distant intergalactic gas clouds. More confirmation of the high presence of helium in distant galaxies was later made by American and Ukrainian astronomers, as noted in the 1999 issue of the *Astrophysical Journal*.[16]

A Confirmed Model and a Confirmed Principle

In the years since the original COBE discoveries, millions of data points of the universe have been mapped annually, which continually adds experimental data to confirm Einstein's principle of general relativity. The big-bang theory has been tested by measuring the expansion speed of the most distant galaxies, and five independent methods have come up with extremely consistent indications that the universe is between 14.6 to 15.1 billion years old.[17] Today, virtually all physicists accept general relativity as an essential law of physics, and the big bang as the model of the origin of the universe. In a 2001 interview, astrophysicist Dr. Hugh Ross noted,

> General relativity is as close to a law of physics as one gets.[18]

Elsewhere Ross further emphasizes the empirical support for general relativity:

> Over the last few decades numerous observational tests have been devised for general relativity. In each case general relativity has passed with flying colors.[19]
>
> For instance, general relativity predicts the rate at which two neutron stars orbiting one another will move closer together. When this phenomenon was observed and measured, general relativity proved accurate to better than a trillionth of a percent precision.
>
> In the words of Roger Penrose, this test result made general relativity "one of the best confirmed principles in all of physics."[20]

With its latest refinements, the big-bang construct is now admired even by atheists who understand the implications of a universe with a beginning. Physicist Lawrence Krauss, a self-described atheist, praises the model as one of *"the most exquisitely designed entities known to man."* [21]

The Dilemma of Physics

Now we have to face a direct contradiction between two laws and principles of physics:

- *The first law of thermodynamics* indicates that the universe must be infinite in duration because neither matter nor energy can ever be added or removed.

- *The principle of general relativity* indicates that the universe had a beginning. Combined with conclusions drawn from exploration of the cosmos, it indicates that the universe is approximately 15 billion years old.

Both simply cannot be right.

———————

Those supporting naturalistic evolution are in a quandary. A universe of infinite duration—like the first law of thermodynamics points to—would, theoretically, allow adequate time for the first living cell to arise. But as soon as a time limit is placed on the age of the universe, there is not nearly enough time (as we have seen in chapter 11). And the empirical evidence we have now from the latest tools of astrophysics supports general relativity, which points to a beginning. Further, theorists who hold to a naturalistic view of the cosmos have no explanation for the conflict between the first law and general relativity.

Those who support intelligent design, though, can point to a logical resolution. If an intelligent designer exists, he could certainly create the universe by using the process we call the "big bang" in a highly precise way (as we will see in the next chapter). Furthermore, a creator could, by definition, *create* matter and energy at the same time he created the first law of thermodynamics. And he could create all the other laws of physics that science has discovered— including the laws that must be obeyed by the incredibly complex cellular systems we've looked at throughout this book.

Seventeen

A Finely Tuned Universe: What Are the Odds?

Most cosmologists and astrophysicists today agree that the big-bang model of the origin of the universe is accurate. Ever since Einstein published his theory of general relativity, more and more of those scientists have also acknowledged, however reluctantly, that a universe with a beginning is very strong evidence for the existence of a "beginner." After all, a beginning demands a cause. And a cause demands a being that can create the cause—perhaps an infinite being, but certainly a being beyond time and space.

Einstein recognized that his theory implied a creator of some type. After Hubble demonstrated in 1929 that some 40 galaxies were indeed receding from one another as the theory predicted, Einstein begrudgingly accepted the "necessity of a beginning" and "the presence of a superior reasoning power." And as we noted in the last chapter, upon receiving the first data about the edges of the universe from the COBE space probe in 1992, project leader George Smoot remarked, "It's like looking at God."[1]*

---

* Interestingly, there is evidence that information about the beginning of the universe and the big-bang model was communicated directly to mankind through a supernatural source long ago. See appendix C.

Resisting the Implication

Astronomer Geoffrey Burbidge, an atheist, was so dismayed by the 1992 findings of the COBE spacecraft and confirming experiments, he complained that "his peers were rushing off to join the 'First Church of the Big Bang.'"[2] Other atheists, recognizing the theological implications, started coming to the fore. In early 1993, the Council for Democratic and Secular Humanism ran an article in their magazine *Free Inquiry* entitled, "Does the Big Bang Prove the Existence of God?"[3] Even the prestigious British journal *Nature* enlisted its physics editor, John Maddox, to write an editorial entitled "Down with the Big Bang." There was no doubt in the minds of all those people about the theistic implications of general relativity and the big bang.

For centuries, Christians have been criticized for relying on a "God of the gaps"—that is, using God to explain what they couldn't figure out otherwise. Often such criticism was deserved. But since the twentieth century the situation has been reversed. Now there is very strong evidence for an intelligent designer, and some evolutionists are attempting to explain it away.

Evidence that We Live in a Finely Tuned Universe

Before we look more closely at some evidence for the perfect design of the universe, let's build a basic framework. The big-bang model indicates that the stars, galaxies, gas clouds, planets—all the components of the universe—developed in a certain sequence. Here are some key points:

1. We can't account for the very first 10^{-43} seconds. This is, of course, an instantaneously short period of time. Researchers are attempting to use quantum physics and *string theory* to determine what might have happened. Perhaps this is when the laws of physics, as we observe them today, were created.

2. The expansion of the universe might be likened to a balloon being blown up. Every point on the balloon would be expanding away from every other point. The original

expansion would have been an incredible release of energy, neutrons, and protons within the very first second.

3. As the universe expanded and its temperature fell, light elements would start to form, including deuterium, helium-3, and helium-4.

4. At about 10,000 years after the big bang, the temperature would have fallen enough that the universe would have been dominated by massive particles, along with the radiation that had been generated earlier. Gravitational forces could begin to take effect between these particles.

5. Background radiation (as discussed in the previous chapter) originated on the *surface of last scattering,* when the temperature of the universe had dropped adequately so that the radiation would no longer interact with the background gas. This occurred about 100,000 years after the origin. The background radiation has propagated itself ever since.

Though the big bang appears to be a completely chaotic event, is there any evidence of a guiding supernatural intelligence who actually planned the specific events right down to the arrangement of stars, galaxies, supernovas, and even planets?

The Anthropic Principle

Almost by accident, astrophysicists started realizing amazing things about the physics of the big bang and how it seemed to set up a perfect environment for life on planet earth. A term for this was coined: the *anthropic principle.* It points to the concept that the development of the universe seems to be aimed at providing an environment suitable for human life.

One of the first things that was noticed was the rate of the expansion of the universe. It was just right for the formation of stars and galaxies. If the rate had been greater, matter would have dispersed too efficiently to form galaxies. No galaxies—then no stars, no sun, and no earth. On the other hand, had the rate been slower, matter would have clumped together so efficiently that it would have collapsed into a high-density "lump" before any stars could form. Again, no stars and no sun—no earth.

Even more significantly, just after the origin event the expansion velocity was modified by two factors:

- *The cosmic mass density.* Physicists have calculated that for physical life to ever be possible at any time in the universe, the overall cosmic mass density must be fine-tuned to a mere 1 part in 10^{60}.

- *The cosmic space energy density.* Likewise, physicists have calculated that the value of the cosmological constant (see page 201) must be exact to 1 part in 10^{120}. Shortly before the cosmological constant was discovered, astrophysicist Lawrence Krauss noted that its addition to the big-bang model "would involve the most extreme fine-tuning problem known in physics."[4]

The odds that just these two aspects of the big bang randomly happened are 1 in 10^{180}—about the same as winning 23 lotteries in a row with a single ticket for each!

Here are some more amazing factors:

- *The speed of light.* The constant of the speed of light—299,792,458 kilometers per second—is critical to the existence of life. A faster speed of light would cause energy ("E" in "$E=mc^2$") to increase dramatically, burning up life on planet earth. A lower "E" would cause things to freeze.

- *The age of the universe when the earth appeared.* The earth had to appear at a certain stage—several generations of giant stars had to have fused enough heavy elements to allow for the proper earth chemistry. Also, the earth had to be located in the right part of the galaxy for life to appear.

- *Small-mass and large-mass stars.* Both are needed in order for life to exist. For this to be possible, the ratio of the electromagnetic force constant to the gravitational force constant must be correct within 1 part in 10^{40}. An increase or decrease in this ratio by only that factor would make life untenable.[5]

Considering just the above points, already the big bang suddenly doesn't look nearly so chaotic, disorganized, or unplanned.

More Evidence for the Anthropic Principle

Once some astrophysicists started discovering the amazing precision of the cosmos, others started seeking additional parameters that might have been preprogrammed into the universe to make an environment suitable for life.

Since that time, about 10 to 15 new critical parameters have been discovered each year. A small change in any one of these would make life impossible. To date, more than 152 have been identified. (More than 120 are listed in appendix A.)

It's often surprising what factors play a part in earth's suitability for human life. Here's a sampling of some of the critical parameters:[6]

- Earth's distance from sun: Too close, too hot for life. Too far, too cold.

- Sun's location relative to center of galaxy: Too close to center, too close to meteor storms. Too far away, too unstable.

- Sun's mass: Key to energy distribution to earth.

- Sun's short-term and long-term luminosity variability: Must be in proper ranges for photosynthesis.

- Tilt of planetary axis: Necessary for seasons. All three forms of water (liquid, ice, and gas) are necessary to maximize life variables.

- Number of moons: Must have one moon for tidal forces, but more than one would create unbearable tidal instability.

- Ratio of oceans to continents: Must be correct to keep global temperature stable (land and water absorb heat at different rates).

○ Position and mass of Jupiter relative to Earth: Jupiter's gravity is critical to life on earth.

○ Atmospheric transparency: Important both for rate of photosynthesis and degree of energy transfer (heat) to earth.

○ Carbon dioxide level: Important for rate of vegetation stabilization.

○ Oxygen level: Important for ozone protection and amount of breathable air for animals.

○ Amount of phosphorus in crust: A critical element for health of bone and muscles.

○ Chlorine quantity in atmosphere: Critical for developing electrolyte balance.

○ Selenium quantity in crust: A critical mineral as an antioxidant.

○ Fluorine quantity in crust: A critical mineral for the body.

○ Quantity of forest and grass fires: Necessary for revitalization of earth nutrients. However, too many would destroy plant–animal balance.

○ Volcanic activity: Necessary for spreading of soil nutrients. However, too much could block out critical sun energy.

From just this partial listing, we can start to see that the conditions on this planet are far from random. A variation in one of them of 10 percent—in some cases as little as one-thousandth of a percent—would make life impossible.

The Probability of the Earth's Characteristics

Astrophysicist Hugh Ross has applied probability theory to the 128 parameters listed in appendix A in the back of this book. Here's a summary of his amazing findings:

1. The probability of all 128 factors being found in any one planet is 1 chance in 10^{166}.

2. The maximum number of planets in the universe is
   10^{22}.[7]

3. Putting these together, there is only 1 chance in 10^{144}
   (10^{166} - 10^{22} = 10^{144}) that any other planet like earth
   exists.

How small is this number? It would be like winning 21 lotteries in a row with a single ticket for each. It would be like taking
all the subatomic particles from almost two universes the size of
ours and randomly picking a preselected particle. Essentially it's
impossible. Therefore, again we find a hard-science calculation
indicating that there is design in life.

———————

So the big bang was not a chaotic explosion. Actually, it looks
like an immense master plan to prepare an environment that precisely fits the needs of human beings and the other living creatures
on earth. Though we've seen the bridge of evolution crumble at
each point, the bridge of purposeful, intelligent design seems to
be able to span the chasm—whether from nonlife to today's 1.7
million species, or from the very moment of the origin of the universe to our present planet, which is exactly equipped to be our
home.

How to Build a Strong Bridge

We've talked a lot about building bridges in this book—from the basics of what makes a strong physical bridge to the analogy of evaluating a theoretical bridge that takes us from the beginning of time to the present.

It's a given that we exist, that the many animal and plant species of the world exist, and that the vast array of the heavens exists. The question is, how did all of this come to be? The evolutionist believes everything came about by natural processes. Others believe that an intelligent designer—be it God or someone else—created things.

The Two Bridges

Our first purpose was to call into question naturalistic presuppositions that have been made primarily since the time of Darwin. A great number of evolutionists have relied on naturalistic

217

assumptions without making a fair, objective evaluation of the facts. (Of course, it could be said of many theologians also that they have failed to weigh all the facts.) Space physicist Wernher von Braun, past director of NASA's Marshall Space Flight Center, sums it up the best:

> I find it as difficult to understand a scientist who does not acknowledge the presence of a superior rationality behind the existence of the universe as it is to comprehend a theologian who would deny the advances of science.[1]

However, the difference has been that the schools, the media, and many people have broadly accepted naturalistic evolution as "science" and, based on incorrect facts and evidence, have separated it from "religion." We've attempted to clarify all the facts and evidence in the hope that everyone can become more aware of the quickly changing world as it relates to the issues of naturalistic evolution and intelligent design.

We should consider that the way we've been teaching naturalistic evolution in our world is every bit as much teaching religion as is teaching the Bible, the Quran, or any other holy book. To see this, all we have to do is start with the definition of God in Webster's dictionary—"the originator of the universe." We find that naturalistic evolution teaches that God was not the originator of the universe—hence it teaches *no* God, or atheism. This is what turned me personally to atheism (for the full story, see my book *A Skeptic's Search for God,* available from Harvest House).

Once we understand that there are strong elements of belief in evolution—belief in incredible, highly improbable events—we can recognize that evolution is every bit as much a religion as it is a theory. And once we fully understand that evolution is a religion, hopefully we can step back and evaluate its likelihood in a more objective, truly scientific way.

Then, our second purpose has been to explore whether there is a different and better way to explain the "givens" of our and the universe's existence. We've evaluated a lot of evidence to see whether it fits better into a framework that includes a *non*naturalistic assumption: that an intelligent designer's involvement may better explain the origin of life and the universe.

Viewpoints from Which to Look at the Bridges

As we've progressed through the book, we've looked at the theories of evolution and intelligent design from a number of different perspectives. Let's take a glance back over the ground we've covered.

- Early on, the *difference between soft science and hard science* was pointed out. Though making observations and conjectures—and looking at dinosaur bones and the fossil record—are fascinating, soft sciences rarely provide conclusive pieces of evidence regarding how events went from point A to point B. Can soft sciences provide clues? Yes. But do they provide hard evidence? No.

- We reviewed the *common myths of evolution* that are still used in textbooks and discussed in the popular media. These myths include that homology is legitimate evidence for common ancestry, or that embryology is evidence of the same. We also looked at some well-known examples that are misleading, such as the famous case of the peppered moth, which is nothing more than microevolution at work; and the Miller–Urey experiments, which falsely lead people to think we have created life in a test tube.

- We looked at the *fossil record* and its lack of the transitional species that were the great hope for evolutionists. Even they recognized this expectation is unfulfilled. Instead, we have fossil evidence of things like the Cambrian explosion, when a vast number of creatures suddenly appeared, with no evidence of previous life forms leading to them. This seems like an introduction of newly created creatures.

- We pointed out that some of the strongest scientific supporters of evolution admitted they do not know how the key transitions of evolution could have taken place. These transitions had to have happened for evolutionary development of the world as we know it today. From the words of evolutionary theorists themselves, we could see that evolution is not a proven scientific fact.

With advances in molecular biology, physics, statistics, information theory, and cosmology, hard evidence has become extremely plentiful. No longer do we have to rely on conjecture. We reviewed just a small portion of the *microbiology of a "typical" cell* and the amazing functions it provides in an incredibly small space, over incredibly short periods of time. Some examples of the cellular motors in the human body were given. These motors go far beyond what evolutionists have ever conceived—for example, the hundreds of ATP motors on each of trillions of mitochondria in your body, which function far more efficiently than any similar man-made machine.

Then we moved into one of the most puzzling areas for evolutionists ever—the issue of the *chirality (molecular orientation) of DNA nucleotides and amino acids.* As we saw, all of the nucleotides need to be right-handed, and all the amino acids, left-handed. For this reason alone, the origin of life by random chance becomes statistically impossible.

Other issues that deny neo-Darwinian evolution were presented, including the *necessary precision of gene sequencing* to properly guide the development of any organism. Likewise, we saw the importance of the *correct selection of amino acids*—that are not only life-specific ones, but ones in precisely the right order to allow proteins to function properly. A rough calculation was made of the probability of the random assembly of first life. We found that it is literally impossible, let alone the vast parade of evolutionary development that supposedly followed.

Mutations, widely claimed by evolutionists to be the mechanism for change, were considered. Problems immediately arose when we noted that mutations are almost never positive. And even when they are positive, the likelihood of their survival is small. Our statistical analysis clearly indicated that it is virtually impossible for mutations to work as a mechanism for change even if positive assumptions are made. More importantly, there is no indication that mutations ever add information to a genome. So using mutations as an explanation for evolutionary transition between species appears to be unreasonable.

Irreducibly complex body systems, especially at the biochemical level, introduce an entirely new area of difficulty for evolutionary theory. It's all but impossible to explain how interdependent parts somehow came together at precisely the same time, in precisely the necessary way, to make a system function. Gradualism, the basis of neo-Darwinism, doesn't work here. It is all or nothing. The odds of the random formation of the many such irreducibly complex systems in the human body are virtually zero.

Nanotechnology was discussed, as well as the recognition of design in molecular biology by evolutionists, who use the words "design" and "machines" regarding biochemical systems. Some of the latest ideas about copying biochemical machines were discussed. With the molecular biology available to us today, it becomes hard to argue against the evidence of design in cellular structure and cellular systems in living creatures.

Before we left the evaluation of living systems, we discussed *information theory* and put the naturalistic evolution and intelligent design concepts through the explanatory filter developed by William Dembski. Seeing the complexity and specificity of living systems led us to the conclusion that their origin is totally unexplainable by a random model or a random model combined with natural selection.

Moving into areas of general physics and the development of the universe itself, we discovered a *contradiction between the first law of thermodynamics and Einstein's principle of general relativity.* Now that we have nearly a hundred years of evidence backing the big-bang theory and general relativity, with the vast majority of evidence coming in the last few years, we are assured that the universe indeed had a beginning. We have been able to calculate a "scientific" age of the universe—about 15 billion years. These parameters essentially mean that the random development of life is a "dead issue." It simply couldn't have happened in such a short time frame.

In our mapping of the heavens, now aided by vast quantities of newly gathered information, we have come to realize that the earth is uniquely designed and situated in the universe specifically for humans (the *anthropic principle*). Every year scientists discover new life-requirements that often can vary only slightly without making life impossible on earth. When the probabilities of all these requirements are considered together, we see that the odds of the existence of another life-specific planet in the universe are virtually nil.

Finally, as we saw the bridge of evolution dismantled piece by piece throughout the book, we were reminded several times that there is one question that evolution simply cannot resolve:

How is life added to chemical compounds?

Where Does the Stronger Bridge Lead Us?

As we see the bridge of evolution crashing into the chasm below, we can see a stronger bridge take its place. It's as if this bridge were made up of beautifully crafted DNA molecules that orchestrate the development of life in an inconceivable symphony.

The molecules in this bridge know miraculously just when to divide a single cell into two...then four...then eight...then sixteen and so on. They know when to start making an arm, a foot, or an eye. And each cell of the resulting living organism knows precisely what atoms it needs precisely when.

So as each day goes by, the symphony of a perfectly directed living creature or plant continues to resound, each particular need being played like a wonderful note of music. There is no guesswork. There is no randomness. There is no neo-Darwinism. Just intricate machines amazingly designed, performing in a most miraculous way. The machines of life we see are far beyond the comprehensible. And they are far beyond any human's ability to design.

Likewise, we see the work of an intelligent designer throughout the heavens themselves. In what has been inappropriately labeled as a "big bang," we can see evidence of an orchestra with billions upon billions of instruments. As the arrangement of galaxies, supernovas, and planets swirled into one incredible crescendo leading to the arrival of life, purpose was in every single step—it was all designed for the support of life on earth.

Those who believe that the intelligent designer is the God of the universe can consider the design that we observe—and measure it as a revelation of his existence. Theologians call this *general revelation*. It is revelation of the existence of God, from his creation. The Bible refers to it:

> Since the creation of the world God's invisible qualities—his eternal power and divine nature—have been clearly seen, being understood from what has been made, so that men are without excuse (Romans 1:20).

We are at a point in scientific inquiry when, for the first time, the evidence of intelligent design is readily apparent in astrophysics and in molecular biology—in the intricate machines built into living organisms. So those scientists who have built their careers—and those others who have built their thinking—on the presupposition of evolution are now faced with a new challenge.

In essence, this challenge means a change in faith from one unseen thing to another. No one has ever seen evolution in action. Nor has anyone ever seen an intelligent designer such as God. Both require faith. Faith in the nothing of evolution leads us to despair. Belief in the God of intelligent design leads us to great hope. Renowned astrophysicist Robert Jastrow illustrates such a quest:

> For the scientist [evolutionist] who has lived by his faith in the power of reason, the story ends like a bad dream. He has scaled the mountain of ignorance; he is about to conquer the highest peak; as he pulls himself over the final rock, he is greeted by a band of theologians who have been sitting there for centuries.[2]

Those who cast off the weights of evolutionary presuppositions can scale that final peak and find peace in an intelligent-designer God—a real God that has beautifully and wonderfully crafted all living things. He's waiting for evolutionists to find him—and the hope he can bring them all.

Appendix A

Some Evidences That a Planet Was Designed to Support Life

Parameter	Estimated probability of galaxy, star, planet, or moon falling in required range for support of life
local abundance and distribution of dark matter	.1
galaxy cluster size	.1
galaxy cluster location	.1
galaxy size	.1
galaxy type	.1
galaxy location	.1
variability of local dwarf galaxy absorption rate	.1
star location relative to galactic center	.2
star distance from corotation circle of galaxy	.005
star distance from closest spiral arm	.1
z-axis extremes of star's orbit	.02
proximity of solar nebula to a supernova eruption	.01
timing of solar nebula formation relative to supernova eruption	.01
number of stars in system	.7
number and timing of close encounters by nearby stars	.01
proximity of close stellar encounters	.1
masses of close stellar encounters	.1

star birth date	.2
star age	.4
star metallicity	.05
star orbital eccentricity	.1
star mass	.001
star luminosity change relative to speciation types and rates	.00001
star color	.4
star carbon-to-oxygen ratio	.01
star space velocity relative to local standard of rest	.05
star short-term luminosity variability	.05
star long-term luminosity variability	.05
number and timing of solar system encounters with interstellar gas clouds	.1
H_3+ production	.1
supernovae rates and locations	.01
white dwarf binary types, rates, and locations	.01
planetary distance from star	.001
inclination of planetary orbit	.5
axis tilt of planet	.3
rate of change of axis tilt	.01
period and size of axis tilt variation	.1
planetary rotation period	.1
rate of change in planetary rotation period	.05
planetary orbit eccentricity	.3
rate of change of planetary orbit eccentricity	.1
rate of change of planetary inclination	.5
period and size of eccentricity variation	.1
period and size of inclination variation	.1
number of moons	.2
mass and distance of moon	.01
surface gravity (escape velocity)	.001
tidal force from sun and moon	.1
magnetic field	.01
rate of change and character of change in magnetic field	.1
albedo (planet reflectivity)	.1
density	.1
thickness of crust	.01
oceans-to-continents ratio	.2
rate of change in oceans-to-continents ratio	.1
global distribution of continents	.3

frequency, timing, and extent of ice ages	.1
frequency, timing, and extent of global snowball events	.1
asteroidal and cometary collision rate	.1
change in asteroidal and cometary collision rates	.1
rate in change in asteroidal and cometary collision rates	.1
mass of body colliding with primordial earth	.002
timing of body colliding with primordial earth	.05
location of body's collision with primordial earth	.05
position and mass of Jupiter relative to earth	.01
major planet eccentricities	.1
major planet orbital instabilities	.05
drift and rate of drift in major planetary distances	.05
number and distribution of planets	.01
atmospheric transparency	.01
atmospheric pressure	.01
atmospheric viscosity	.1
atmospheric electrical discharge rate	.01
atmospheric temperature gradient	.01
carbon dioxide level in atmosphere	.01
rate of change in carbon dioxide level in atmosphere	.1
rate of change in water vapor level in atmosphere	.01
rate of change in methane level in early atmosphere	.01
oxygen quantity in atmosphere	.01
chlorine quantity in atmosphere	.1
cobalt quantity in crust	.1
arsenic quantity in crust	.1
copper quantity in crust	.1
boron quantity in crust	.1
fluorine quantity in crust	.1
iodine quantity in crust	.1
manganese quantity in crust	.1
nickel quantity in crust	.1
phosphorus quantity in crust	.1
tin quantity in crust	.1
zinc quantity in crust	.1
molybdenum quantity in crust	.05
vanadium quantity in crust	.1
chromium quantity in crust	.1
selenium quantity in crust	.1
iron quantity in oceans	.1

tropospheric ozone quantity	.01
stratospheric ozone quantity	.01
mesospheric ozone quantity	.01
water vapor level in atmosphere	.01
oxygen-to-nitrogen ratio in atmosphere	.1
quantity of greenhouse gases in atmosphere	.01
rate of change of greenhouse gases in atmosphere	.01
quantity of forest and grass fires	.01
quantity of sea salt aerosols	.1
soil mineralization	.1
quantity of anaerobic bacteria in the oceans	.01
quantity of aerobic bacteria in the oceans	.01
quantity of decomposer bacteria in soil	.01
quantity of mycorrhizal fungi in soil	.01
quantity of nitrifying microbes in soil	.01
quantity and timing of vascular plant introductions	.01
quantity, timing, and placement of carbonate-producing animals	.00001
quantity, timing, and placement of methanogens	.00001
quantity of soil sulfur	.1
quantity of sulfur in planet core	.1
quantity of silicon in planet core	.1
quantity of water at subduction zones in the crust	.01
hydration rate of subducted minerals	.1
tectonic activity	.05
rate of decline in tectonic activity	.1
volcanic activity	.1
rate of decline in volcanic activity	.1
viscosity at planet core boundaries	.01
viscosity of lithosphere	.2
biomass to comet infall ration	.01
regularity of comet infall	.1
number, intensity, and location of hurricanes	.02

dependency factors estimate	1,000,000,000,000,000,000,000.
longevity requirements estimate	.0000001

probability for occurrence of all 128 parameters $\approx 10^{-166}$

maximum possible number of planets in universe $\approx 10^{22}$

Summary

For all these factors to come together in a single planet is less than one chance in 10^{144}. Earth was clearly designed for human beings, and the odds of the existence of another such planet are nil, now that we have a defined boundary for and an estimated number of potential planets in the universe.

Note that different categories of life would be affected differently by variation in the parameters. Some might survive a certain change better; some, worse. For example, unicellular, low-metabolism life is more susceptible to radiation damage and has a very low molecular repair rate. The six categories are

1. unicellular, low-metabolism life with a short life span

2. unicellular, low-metabolism life with a long life span

3. unicellular, high-metabolism life with a short life span

4. unicellular, high-metabolism life with a high life span

5. advanced life with a short life span

6. advanced life with a long life span

For more information on this and other scientific facts supporting the existence of a God of the universe, contact Reasons to Believe, PO Box 5978, Pasadena, CA 91117, or call (626) 335-1480. See also their Web site: www.reasons.org.

The information in this appendix comes from research by Dr. Hugh Ross and is adapted from Hugh Ross, *The Creator and the Cosmos*, 3rd edition (Colorado Springs, CO: NavPress, 2001), pages 195–198. © 1993, 1995, 2001 Reasons to Believe. Used by permission of NavPress (www.navpress.com). All rights reserved.

How Old Are the Earth and the Universe?

Throughout this book we've referred to the universe as being about 15 billion years old. This is the number widely used by scientists today based on the latest information gathered. It is based on analysis of at least three factors:[1]

1. *The redshift.* This is a measurement of the velocities and distances of many different distant galaxies as they move away from the big bang. It calculates the time it would have taken them to get to their present locations from the original center.

2. *Globular clusters.* The brightness and temperature of distant stars can be measured and plotted on a "Hertzsprung–Russell" diagram. The ages of clusters (groupings of stars) can be determined by observing where groupings leave the "main-line sequence" of star development.

3. *The half-lives of radioactive elements* that are abundant in galaxies at the outer edges of the universe (for example, thorium-232) can be measured by nuclear chronometers.

These methods consistently indicate that the universe is approximately 15 billion years old. Because they have been developed over many years and have been supported by thousands of observations, the methods are highly trusted.

Dating the Earth

Determining the age of the earth raises several problems. For example, the crust of the earth today is not the same as the original crust, and therefore it cannot lead us to a direct measurement.

One thing we can be certain of is this: The earth is at least as old as the geological events that could only have happened on it once it was completed—such as volcanic eruptions. Based on this method of measurement, a reliable minimum age would be in the hundreds of millions of years.

Radiometric Dating

Radiometric dating provides the major means of estimating the age of the earth. We should note that there are more than 40 types of radiometric dating. But all of them use essentially the same technique to examine rocks with radioactive elements. The number of *daughter atoms* present (those produced by radioactive decay) are measured in proportion to the number of *parent atoms* remaining (those that still have their original radioactivity). These are known as *half-life* measurements. The number of parent atoms decreases exponentially at each point in time.[2]

The accuracy of radiometric dating is very high. The half-lives of most radioactive isotopes used for dating are known to within plus-or-minus 2 percent. (It is critical for accuracy that the right method of dating is used for the right material. When anomalies appear, materials are often retested using a different method to check for agreement.)

Some of the kinds of events that radiometric dating is best at determining are, for instance, the time that has passed since the cooling of molten lava from a volcano; the end of a period of meta-morphic heating (in particular, heating to greater than 1000 degrees); or the time since the death of a living creature (in this case, carbon dating is generally used). And recently, methods have been deployed that can be used to date even certain types of sedi-mentary rock. This is critical because many fossils are found in this kind of rock.

As mentioned, the dating of the earth itself is difficult since the early crust is long vanished. However, rocks have been found—on 5 different continents—that date to between 3.8 and 3.9 billion years old, and they contain minerals dating to 4.1 to 4.2 billion years old.[3] Because the rocks are believed to have been formed on earth, not as meteorites in outer space, this would seem to set a lower boundary for the earth's age. However, this is still not an absolute certainty.

"The most direct means for calculating the Earth's age from core samples is a Pb/Pb [lead–lead] isochron age, derived from samples of the Earth and meteorites. This involves measurement of three isotopes of lead (Pb-206, Pb-207, and either Pb-208 or Pb-204)."[4] This methodology has resulted in an empirical age esti-mate of 4.6 billion years.

The Reliability of Radiometric Dating

The vast body of science accepts radiometric dating as reli-able. In fact, several hundred laboratories around the world are active using radioactive-dating methods. For instance, in the year 2001, more than a thousand articles on radiometric dating were published in recognized scientific journals. Hundreds of thou-sands of dates have been measured and published in the last 50 years—and when it was appropriate to corroborate these dates using different methods, there was very precise agreement in the measurements.

Sometimes the accuracy of radiometric dating is questioned because of anomalies that occasionally occur. It's then suggested that the entire methodology is flawed. This would be like claiming that penicillin doesn't work at all just because some patients are allergic to it. However, in such a case, penicillin might be the incor-rect drug for a certain individual. A doctor would then prescribe an appropriate drug for that patient. Likewise, a particular dating method might be the wrong one for a specific situation or type of material. A researcher would then retest the material using the correct dating method.[1]*

Viewpoints About the Age of the Earth and the Universe

Many scientists—who also believe in the God of the Bible—firmly believe that the universe is about 15 billion years old. Furthermore, they believe that this dating is consistent with the original Hebrew of the Scriptures in Genesis chapter 1. Likewise, many theologians who believe in the Genesis record also accept that the universe is about 15 billion years old. In fact, the number of people who understand that the Bible is consistent with the scientific record is rapidly increasing, according to Craig Hazen, PhD, director of Biola University's Christian Apologetics program and coordinator of periodic conferences on creation.[5]

It's sometimes argued that a 15-billion-year-old universe contradicts the biblical record in the book of Genesis. However, experts in analysis of the original Hebrew text indicate that the original wording allows some latitude—enough so that the original language can be consistent with either a younger or an older age of the universe.[6]

---

* I encourage anyone who has concerns about the reliability of radiometric dating to read *Radiometric Dating: A Christian Perspective* by Dr. Roger C. Wiens.

Dr. Wiens holds a PhD in physics, with a minor in geology. His doctoral dissertation was on the subject of isotope ratios in meteorites, including surface exposure dating. He was employed at the California Institute of Technology's Division of Geological and Planetary Sciences when he wrote the first edition of *Radiometric Dating* (1994; a revised version was written in 2002), and is presently employed in the Space and Atmospheric Sciences Group at the Los Alamos National Laboratory.

Radiometric Dating can be obtained by writing or e-mailing as follows:

Dr. Roger C. Wiens
941 Estates Drive
Los Alamos, NM 87544
RWiens@Prodigy.Net

It can also be found on the Internet, at
<http://www.asa3.org/ASA/resources/Wiens.html>.

Further, it's also been suggested that a multibillion-year age for the universe has been promoted by science in order to afford enough time for evolution. But as we've seen throughout this book, it is impossible that the vast complexity of even the simplest cell could have arisen randomly within that time frame—let alone the vast parade of evolutionary development theorized by neo-Darwinists.

Therefore, even if someone holds the viewpoint that the universe is only about 10,000 years old, the conclusions drawn in this book are every bit as valid. After all, if evolution is impossible within 15 billion years, it's certainly far less likely in only 10,000 years.

Principles for Considering the Age-of-the-Universe Issue

Theologians refer to two vitally important ways that God reveals himself to human beings—*general revelation* and *special revelation*. Since God is one, and since he is unchanging, there can be no contradiction between the two.

General Revelation

God reveals himself to us through his creation. In other words, we can "see God" as we acknowledge the vastness of the heavens with all their starry splendor. We can "see God" in what he's provided for us—the sun for heat, water to drink, food to eat, material for shelter. We can "see God" in the strength of the lion, the delicacy of the butterfly, or the scent of a beautiful flower.

The Bible emphatically states that God is revealed through his creation:

> The heavens declare the glory of God; the skies proclaim the work of his hands (Psalm 19:1).
>
> Since the creation of the world God's invisible qualities—his eternal power and divine nature—have been clearly seen, being understood from what has been made (Romans 1:20).

Special Revelation

This is the revelation of God through his divinely inspired written Word, the Bible. Just as with the magnificence of creation, we can marvel at the insights about God that are revealed in this unique book. God reveals his nature, his plan, and his guidelines. Furthermore, God provides ways to test the veracity of the biblical text—the most important one being 100-percent-perfect prophecy that can be proven to be statistically impossible without divine inspiration.

The biblical authors leave no doubt that they consider the Bible to be 100 percent from God, specially revealed by him:

> All Scripture is God-breathed and is useful for teaching, rebuking, correcting and training in righteousness, so that the man of God may be thoroughly equipped for every good work (2 Timothy 3:16-17).

God would not contradict himself or his own nature. So when we consider the substantial amount of empirical evidence for a multibillion-year-old universe, we need to keep in mind that general revelation and special revelation must be consistent. God does not deceive us. He would not make things "look old" to cause us to jump to the wrong conclusions. Moreover, God expects us to use our *minds* as an essential part of loving him, as we see in the "greatest commandment":

> Love the Lord your God with all your heart and with all your soul and with all your *mind* and with all your strength (Mark 12:30, emphasis added).

In Summary

God has given human beings minds to study his creation and marvel at his handiwork. What is revealed to us in his creation is consistent with the account of creation contained in the book of Genesis.

Whether we hold to a 15-billion-year-old age for the universe—or some shorter time frame—it makes absolutely no difference in evaluating the evidence in this book.

- Specifically, there is not nearly enough time for even the first, simplest cell of life to be formed randomly.

- Therefore, since the first cell of life could not have come about by chance, the remaining claims of evolutionary theorists are moot. And even if a first cell could have developed, again, there was not enough time for all the necessary transitions to occur randomly—the many transitions that would have to have happened to bring about the existence of the many different species on earth today.

Appendix C

The Original Source of Evidence for a "Beginner"

The Bible itself, interestingly, is strong evidence for a being—an intelligent designer—from beyond time and space. (See my earlier book, *A Skeptic's Search for God,* for more about this.) A number of examples in the Bible talk about God existing before time began:

- "The hope of eternal life, which God, who does not lie, promised before the beginning of time..." (Titus 1:2).

- "This grace was given us in Christ Jesus before the beginning of time..." (2 Timothy 1:9).

- "You [the Father] loved me before the creation of the world" (Jesus, in John 17:24).

- "He [God the Father] chose us in him [Jesus Christ] before the creation of the world" (Ephesians 1:4).

- "He [Christ] was chosen before the creation of the world" (1 Peter 1:20).

The Bible also agrees with two other key aspects of the big bang: 1) There was a beginning, and 2) things were created by an intelligent designer (God):

- "In the beginning God created the heavens and the earth" (Genesis 1:1).

- "Through him [the Word, Jesus Christ] all things were made; without him nothing was made that has been made" (John 1:3).

- "By him [Jesus Christ] all things were created: things in heaven and on earth, visible and invisible, whether thrones or powers or rulers or authorities; all things were created by him and for him. He is before all things, and in him all things hold together" (Colossians 1:16-17).

The Bible also speaks of the stretching out of the heavens, as indicated in the expanding universe of the big-bang model:

- "This is what God the LORD says—he who created the heavens and stretched them out…" (Isaiah 42:5).

- "…The LORD your Maker, who stretched out the heavens and laid the foundations of the earth" (Isaiah 51:13).

- "God made the earth by his power; he founded the world by his wisdom and stretched out the heavens by his understanding" (Jeremiah 10:12).

The big bang confirms the Bible and firmly closes the door on evolution. Reason number one, as we've seen, is that the big-bang model, along with empirical discoveries about the age of the universe (see appendix B), shows that there was not nearly enough time for the components of the very first cell to come together randomly.

Notes

Things Aren't Always the Way They Appear

1. The *Global Biodiversity Assesment* of the United Nations Enviromental Program (UNEP) estimates the number of described species at approximately 1.75 million. Estimates of the number of unidentified species range from 10 million to more than 100 million. (See Brian Handwerk, "Team Races to Catalog Every Species on Earth," *National Geographic News*, March 5, 2002, p. 1. Accessed at <http://news.nationalgeographic.com/news/2002/03/0305_0305_allspecies.html>.)

Chapter 1—Flaws in the Structure

1. L. Harrison Matthews, introduction to Charles Darwin, *On the Origin of the Species* (reprint, London: J. M. Dent and Sons, Ltd., 1971), p. xi, as cited in Duane T. Gish, *Evolution: the Fossils Still Say No!* (El Cajon, CA: Institute for Creation Research, 1995), p. 5.

2. John Maynard Smith and Eors Szathmary, *The Origins of Life* (New York: Oxford University Press, Inc., 2000), p. 15.

3. Charles Darwin, *On the Origin of the Species*, reprint of 1st ed. (Cambridge, MA: Harvard Press, 1964), p. 95.

4. Darwin, p. 172.

5. Maynard Smith and Szathmary, p. 6, emphasis added.

6. Dr. Lee Spetner, *Not By Chance* (Brooklyn, NY: 1998, The Judaica Press, Inc.), p. 162, emphasis added. He is quoting from p. 43 of *The Blind Watchmaker*.

7. Sir Frederick Hoyle, as cited in Chuck Missler, *The Creator Beyond Time and Space* (Costa Mesa, CA: The Word for Today, 1996), p. 60.

8. R. B. Goldschmidt, *American Scientist* 40:84 (1952), as cited in Duane Gish, *Evolution: The Fossils Still Say No!* (El Cajon, CA: 1995, Institute for Creation Research), p. 1.

9. Goldschmidt, as cited in Gish, p. 3.

10. Stephen Jay Gould, "Is a New and General Theory of Evolution Emerging?" *Paleobiology* 6, no. 1 (1980): pp. 119-30, as cited by Michael Ruse, ed., *But Is It Science?* (Amherst, NY: 1996, Prometheus Books), p. 190.

11. Michael Gross, PhD, *Travels to the Nanoworld* (Cambridge, MA: Perseus Publishing, 1999).

12. Spetner, p. 209.

241

Chapter 2—Steps to Span the Gap
1. Richard A. Swenson, M.D., *More Than Meets the Eye* (Colorado Springs, CO: NavPress, 2000), pp. 17-18.
2. David M. Baughan, M.D., "Contemporary Scientific Principles and Family Medicine," *Family Medicine,* January/February 1987, p. 42; as cited in Swenson, p. 18.
3. John Tyndall, as quoted in Shirley A. Jones, (ed.), *The Mind of God and Other Musings: The Wisdom of Science* (San Rafael, CA: New World Library, 1994), pp. 116-17; as cited in Swenson, p. 18.
4. Dr. Gary Ott, M.D., Surgical Director at Providence Heart Institute, Portland, Oregon. Personal interview, University of California at Irvine, November 7, 2001.
5. John Maynard Smith and Eors Szathmary, *The Origins of Life* (New York: Oxford University Press, Inc., 2000), p. 11.

Chapter 3—Hard Evidence Versus Soft Evidence
1. Dr. Lee Spetner, *Not By Chance* (Brooklyn, NY: The Judaica Press, Inc., 1998), p. 95.
2. *Earth Science,* California ed. (Woodland Hills, CA: Glencoe/McGraw-Hill, 2001).
3. *Earth Science,* p. 383.
4. *Earth Science,* p. 391.
5. *Earth Science,* p. 395.
6. Robert Wright, "Science and the Original Sin," *Time* magazine, October 26, 1996, p. 76.

Chapter 4—Observation: Examining Things Logically
1. Richard A. Swenson, M.D., *More Than Meets the Eye—Fascinating Glimpses of God's Power and Design* (Colorado Springs, CO: NavPress, 2000), p. 21.
2. Gerald L. Schroeder, *The Hidden Face of God: How Science Reveals the Ultimate Truth* (New York, NY: The Free Press, 2001), p. 189.

Chapter 5—The Myths of Evolution
1. "Mythology," World Book Encyclopedia, vol. 13 (Chicago, IL: World Book, Inc., 1988), p. 978.
2. Charles Darwin, *On the Origin of the Species* (Cambridge, MA: Harvard University Press, 1964), pp. 413-14.
3. Dr. Lee Spetner, *Not By Chance* (Brooklyn, NY: The Judaica Press, Inc., 1988), p. 141.
4. Ernst Mayr, *Principles of Systematic Zoology (*1953), as cited by Richard Milton, *Shattering the Myths of Darwinism* (Rochester, VT: Park Street Press, 1997), p. 116.
5. As cited in Jonathan Wells, *Icons of Evolution: Science or Myth?* (Washington D.C.: Regnery Publishing, Inc., 2000), p. 31.
6. Darwin, p. 302.
7. Wells, p. 37.
8. Wells, pp. 81-109.

Chapter 6—The Fossil Record
1. William A. Shear, "Millipedes," *American Scientist,* vol. 87 (May/June 1999), p. 234.
2. National Park Service, Geologic Resources Division, "Geology Fieldnotes, Florissant Fossil Beds National Monument, Colorado"; <http://www.aqd.nps.gov/grd/parks/fifo/>; accessed on 11/21/01.

3. "Rare Fossilized Jellyfish Found," January 25, 2002; Andrew Bridges, AP Science Writer, <http://daily news.yahoo.com/h/ap/20020125/sc/fossil jellyfish 1.html>; accessed on 1/28/02.

4. Charles Darwin, *On the Origin of the Species* (Cambridge, MA: Harvard University Press, 2000), p. 95.

5. Darwin, p. 171.

6. Darwin, p. 172.

7. The Brown University News Bureau, February 25, 1999; <http://brown.edu/Administration/News Bureau/1998-99/98-077.html>; accessed on 12/17/01.

8. Mark Ridley, *New Scientist* 90:830 (1981); as cited in Duane T. Gish, PhD, *Creation Scientists Answer Their Critics* (El Cajon, CA: Institute for Creation Research, 1993), p. 113.

9. T.N. George, *Science Progress* 48:1 (1960); as cited in Gish, *Creation Scientists*, p. 113.

10. Michael Denton, *Evolution: A Theory in Crisis* (Chevy Chase, MD: Adler & Adler, 1997).

11. G.G. Simpson, *Tempo and Mode in Evolution* (New York: Columbia University Press, 1944), p. 105; as cited in Duane T. Gish, *Evolution: The Fossils Still Say No!* (El Cajon, CA: Institute for Creation Research, 1995), p. 334.

12. Simpson, p. 107; as cited in Gish, *Evolution*, p. 334.

13. Jeffrey H. Schwartz, *Sudden Origins* (Hoboken, NJ: John Wiley & Sons, 1999), p. 89; as cited in Genesis Park: "Dinosaurs: Living Evidence of a Powerful Creator (www.genesispark.org), Genesis Park Exhibit Hall, "Room 3—The Story of the Fossils"; <www.genesispark.org/genpark/gaps/gaps.htm>. Used by permission.

14. David B. Kitts, "Paleontology and Evolutionary Theory," *Evolution*, vol. 28, 1974, p. 467; as cited in Genesis Park. Used by permission.

15. Cited in David Raup, "Geology," *New Scientist*, vol. 90 (1981), p. 832; as cited in Genesis Park. Used by permission.

16. Niles Eldredge, *The Myths of Human Evolution* (New York: Columbia University Press, 1982), p. 59; as cited in Genesis Park. Used by permission.

17. Stephen J. Gould, "Is a New and General Theory of Evolution Emerging?" *Paleobiology*, vol. 6 (1980), p. 40; as cited in Genesis Park. Used by permission.

18. Donald Lindsay, "Speciation by Punctuated Equilibrium": University of Colorado Computer Science Department Web site (<http://www.cs.colorado.edu/~lindsay/creation/punk_eek.html>).

19. Steven M. Stanley, *The New Evolutionary Timetable: Fossils, Genes, and the Origin of Species* (New York: Basic Books, 1981), p. 99; as cited in Genesis Park. Used by permission.

20. Donald R. Prothero, PhD, "Punctuated Equilibrium at Twenty: A Paleontological Perspective," *Skeptic*, vol. 1, no. 3 (Fall 1992), pp. 38-47.

21. Gareth Cook, the *Boston Globe;* as reported in the *Orange County Register,* July 11, 2002, p. 1.

22. Cook, as reported in the *Orange County Register.*

Chapter 7—From Atoms to the First Cell
1. John Maynard Smith and Eors Szathmary, *The Origins of Life* (New York: Oxford University Press, Inc., 1999), p. 17.

2. Maynard Smith and Szathmary, p. 19, emphasis added.

3. Maynard Smith and Szathmary, p. 16.

4. Maynard Smith and Szathmary, p. 33.

5. Maynard Smith and Szathmary, p. 34.

6. Christian de Duve, "Clues from Present-Day Biology: The Thioester World" in A. Brack, ed., *The Molecular Origins of Life* (Cambridge, UK: Cambridge University Press, 1998); as cited in Michael Ruse, ed., *But Is it Science?* (Amherst, NY: Prometheus Books, 1996), p. 219.

7. Maynard Smith and Szathmary, p. 46.

8. Maynard Smith and Szathmary, p. 44.

9. James P. Ferris, "Catalyzed RNA Synthesis for the RNA World," in Michael Ruse, ed. *But Is it Science?* (Amherst, NY: 1996, Prometheus Books), p. 255.

10. Ferris, in Ruse, ed., p. 257.

11. Robert Shapiro, PhD, New York University faculty resume, New York University Web site: <www.nyu.edu/pages/chemistry/Faculty/shapiro.html>, emphasis added.

Chapter 8—From the First Cell to 1.7 Million Species
1. John Maynard Smith and Eors Szathmary, *The Origins of Life* (New York: Oxford University Press, Inc. 1999), p. 50.

2. Maynard Smith and Szathmary, p. 60.

3. Maynard Smith and Szathmary, p. 55.

4. Maynard Smith and Szathmary, p. 18.

5. Maynard Smith and Szathmary, p. 81.

6. Maynard Smith and Szathmary, p. 34.

7. R.A. Fisher, *The Genetical Theory of Natural Selection*, 2nd ed. (New York: Dover, 1958); as cited in Dr. Lee Spetner, *Not By Chance* (Brooklyn, NY: The Judaica Press, Inc., 1998), p. 56.

8. Maynard Smith and Szathmary, p. 125.

9. Maynard Smith and Szathmary, p. 133.

10. Maynard Smith and Szathmary, pp. 141,143.

11. Maynard Smith and Szathmary, pp. 165,166.

Chapter 9—The Complexity of Living Cells
1. *World Book Encyclopedia*, vol. 3 (Chicago: World Book, Inc., 1988), p. 328.

2. Dr. Lee Spetner, *Not by Chance* (Brooklyn, NY: The Judaica Press, Inc., 1998), p. 30.

3. Mahlon Hoagland and Bert Dodson, *The Way Life Works* (New York: Three Rivers Press, 1998), p. 15.

4. Gerald L. Schroeder, *The Hidden Face of God* (New York: The Free Press, 2001), p. 189.

5. Richard A. Swenson, M.D., *More Than Meets the Eye: Fascinating Glimpses of God's Power and Design* (Colorado Springs, CO: NavPress, 2000), p. 20. Used by permission.

6. Swenson, pp. 17-18. Used by permission.

7. "Each of the trillions of living cells in the body has an electrical potential difference across the cell membrane. This is a result of an imbalance of the positively and negatively charged ions on the inside and outside of the cell wall. The resultant potential difference is about 0.1 V, but because of the very thin cell wall it may produce an electric field as

large as 10^7 V/m, an electric field that is much larger than the electric field near a high voltage power line." (John R. Cameron, James G. Skofronick, and Roderick M. Grant, *Physics of the Body* [Madison, WI: Medical Physics Publishing, 1999], p. 38.); as cited in Swenson, p. 188. Used by permission.

8. David Rosevear, "The Myth of Chemical Evolution," *Impact,* July 1999, p. iv; as cited in Swenson, p. 188. Used by permission.

9. Rosevear, p. iv; as cited in Swenson, p. 188. Used by permission.

10. Mark Caldwell, "The Clock in the Cell," *Discover,* October 1998, p. 36; as cited in Swenson, p. 188. Used by permission.

11. Swenson, p. 21. Used by permission.

12. Spetner, p. 30.

13. Swenson, p. 65. Used by permission.

14. Swenson., p. 63. Used by permission.

15. Schroeder, p. 189.

16. This and previous bullet points from Swenson, pp. 23,24,26,28,29,30,32,33. Used by permission.

17. John K. Stevens, "Reverse Engineering the Brain," *Byte,* April 1985, pp. 287-99; as cited in Swenson, p. 34. Used by permission.

18. This and other bullet points after note 17 from Swenson, pp. 34,36,37,38,39,40. Used by permission.

Chapter 10—Chirality: There's No Solution in Sight
1. Mahlon Hoagland and Bert Dodson, *The Way Life Works* (New York: Three Rivers Press, 1998), p. 88.

2. Michael Denton, *Evolution: A Theory in Crisis* (Bethesda, MD: Alder and Alder Publications, Inc., 1986), p. 235.

3. Christian de Duve, "Clues from Present-Day Biology in the Thioester World," *The Molecular Origins of Life,* André Brack, ed. (Cambridge, UK: The Cambridge University Press, 1998), p. 222.

4. Alan W. Schwartz, "Origins of the RNA World," Brack, ed., p. 247.

5. J. Cohen, "Getting All Turned Around over the Origins of Life on Earth," *Science,* vol. 267 (1995), pp. 1265-66; as cited in Jonathan Sarfati, "Origin of Life: the Chirality Problem," Answers in Genesis Web site (www.answersingenesis.org).

6. University of California at Davis Web site (www.ucdavis.edu).

7. "Lugodoc's Theory of the Origin of Life on Earth—or the Artificial Origin of DNA," <www.lugodoc.demon.co.uk/lugodoc/rant02.htm>.

8. "Lugodoc's Theory."

9. R.F. Service, "Chemistry: Does Life's Handedness Come from Within?" *Science,* vol. 286 (1999): pp. 1282-83.

Chapter 11—The Probability of the Random Origin of the First Living Cell
1. Marcel P. Schutzenberger, "Algorithms and the New Darwinian Theory of Evolution," as cited in John Ankerberg and John Weldon, "Rational Inquiry and the Force of Scientific Data: Are New Horizons Emerging?" *The Creation Hypothesis: Scientific Evidence for an Intelligent Designer,* J.P. Moreland, ed. (Downers Grove, IL: InterVarsity, 1994), p.

274; as cited in Richard A. Swenson, M.D., *More Than Meets the Eye—Fascinating Glimpses of God's Power and Design* (Colorado Springs, CO: NavPress, 2000), p. 69. Used by permission.

2. Harold Morowitz, as cited in Hugh Ross, *The Creator and the Cosmos: How the Greatest Scientific Discoveries of the Century Reveal God* (Colorado Springs, CO: NavPress, 1995), p. 149.

3. Edward Argyle, "Chance and Origin of Life," *Extraterrestrials—Where are They?* Ben Zuckerman and Michael H. Hart, eds. (Cambridge, England: Cambridge University Press, 1995), p. 131; as cited in Fred Heeren, *Show Me God: What the Message from Space Is Telling Us About God* (Wheeling, IL: Day Star Publications, 1998), p. 61.

4. John Horgan, as quoted in Gerald L. Schroeder, *The Science of God: The Convergence of Scientific and Biblical Wisdom* (New York: Broadway Books, 1997), p. 142; as cited in Swenson, p. 70. Used by permission.

5. Fred Hoyle and Chandra Wickramasinghe, *Evolution from Space* (London: J.M. Dent and Sons, 1981), p. 24; as cited in Heeren.

6. David Foster, as quoted in Heeren, p. 68; as cited in Swenson, pp. 70-71. Used by permission.

7. Hoyle and Wickramasinghe, p. 148; as cited in Heeren.

8. Schroeder, p. 93; as cited in Swenson, p. 71. Used by permission.

9. Carl Sagan and Francis Crick, as quoted in Ankerberg and Weldon, in J.P. Moreland, ed., p. 272; as cited in Swenson, pp. 70-71. Used by permission.

10. Stephen C. Meyer, "The Message in the Microcosm: DNA and the Death of Materialism," *Cosmic Pursuit*, Fall 1997, pp. 41-42; as cited in Swenson, p. 72, emphasis added. Used by permission.

11. Dr. David Whitehouse, "Is Life Just Genes?" *BBC News*, December 9, 1999 (<http://news.bbc.co.uk/1/hi/sci/tech/556958.stm>).

12. C. Thaxton, W. Bradley, R. Olsen, "The Mystery of Life's Origin"; in Mark Eastman, M.D., and Chuck Missler, *The Creator Beyond Time and Space* (Costa Mesa, CA: The Word for Today, 1996), pp. 44-45.

13. Michael Denton, *Evolution: A Theory in Crisis* (Bethesda, MD: Adler and Adler, 1986), p. 262.

14. Eastman and Missler, pp. 52-53.

Chapter 12—Mutations: A Faulty Mechanism
1. *Science Daily*, Web posting of the University of Texas at Austin, 1/10/2002.

2. John Maynard Smith and Eors Szathmary, *The Origins of Life* (New York: The Oxford University Press, Inc., 2000), p. 1.

3. Mahlon Hoagland and Bert Dodson, *The Way Life Works* (New York: Three Rivers Press, 1998), p. 79.

4. Francisco J. Ayala, "The Mechanisms of Evolution," in *But Is It Science?* Michael Ruse, ed. (Amherst, NY: Prometheus Books, 1996), p. 135.

5. *World Book Encyclopedia*, vol. 13 (Chicago: World Book, Inc., 1987), p. 973.

6. Maynard Smith and Szathmary, p. 1.

7. Hoagland and Dodson, p. 79.

8. Ayala, in Ruse, ed., p. 129.

9. *World Book,* p. 973.

10. Fred Hoyle, *The Mathematics of Evolution* (Memphis, TN: Acorn Press, 1999), p. 98.

11. Hoyle, pp. 135-36.

12. Hoyle, p. 105.

13. As cited in Dr. Lee Spetner, *Not By Chance: Shattering the Modern Theory of Evolution* (Brooklyn, NY: The Judaica Press, Inc., 1998), p. 54. Used by permission of Judaica Press, Inc., www.judaicapress.com.

14. T.K. Gartner and E. Orias, University of Santa Barbara, 1966; in Spetner, p. 131.

15. Spetner, pp. 139-41. Used by permission.

16. Spetner, p. 143. Used by permission.

17. Spetner, p. 146. Used by permission.

18. Spetner, p. 148. Used by permission.

19. Spetner, p. 150. The references are to Lerner et al., 1964; Wu et al., 1968; Rigby et al., 1974; Burleigh et al., 1974; Inderlied and Morlock, 1977; Thompson and Krawiec, 1983. Used by permission.

20. Spetner, pp. 94-103. Used by permission.

21. Fersht, 1981; Drake, 1969, 1991; as cited in Spetner, pp. 39,92. Used by permission.

22. Stebbins, 1966; as cited in Spetner, p. 97. Used by permission.

23. As cited in Spetner, p. 102. Used by permission.

24. Spetner, p. 103. Used by permission.

Chapter 13—Irreducible Complexity: A Major Transitional Problem

1. Michael Behe, *Darwin's Black Box* (New York: The Free Press, 1996), p. 39. © 1996 by Michael J. Behe. By permission of The Free Press, a Division of Simon & Schuster Adult Publishing Group.

2. Frances Hitching, *The Neck of the Giraffe* (London: Pan, 1982), p. 68; as cited in Behe, p. 37. © 1996 by Michael J. Behe. By permission of The Free Press, a Division of Simon & Schuster Adult Publishing Group.

3. Richard Dawkins, *The Blind Watchmaker* (London: W. W. Norton, 1985), p. 81.

4. Behe, pp. 18-20. © 1996 by Michael J. Behe. By permission of The Free Press, a Division of Simon & Schuster Adult Publishing Group.

5. Behe, pp. 74-97. © 1996 by Michael J. Behe. By permission of The Free Press, a Division of Simon & Schuster Adult Publishing Group.

6. Russell Doolittle, "The Evolution of Vertebrate Blood Coagulation: A Case of Yin and Yang," *Thrombosis and Haemostasis,* vol. 70 (1993), pp. 24-28; as cited in Behe, pp. 74-97. © 1996 by Michael J. Behe. By permission of The Free Press, a Division of Simon & Schuster Adult Publishing Group.

7. Behe, p. 93. © 1996 by Michael J. Behe. By permission of The Free Press, a Division of Simon & Schuster Adult Publishing Group.

8. Behe, p. 91. © 1996 by Michael J. Behe. By permission of The Free Press, a Division of Simon & Schuster Adult Publishing Group.

9. TPA has a total of five domains. Two domains, however, are of the same type. (Behe, pp. 74-93. © 1996 by Michael J. Behe. By permission of The Free Press, a Division of Simon & Schuster Adult Publishing Group.)

Chapter 14—Nanotechnology: Engineers Copy Our Own Cellular Machines

1. See note 8 for chapter 9.

2. See note 7 for chapter 9.

3. See note 10 for chapter 9.

4. See note 16 for chapter 9.

5. See note 18 for chapter 9.

6. See note 16 for chapter 9.

7. See note 17 for chapter 9.

8. See note 18 for chapter 9.

9. Michael Gross, *Travels to the Nanoworld: Miniature Machinery in Nature and Technology* (Cambridge, MA: Perseus, 1999), p. 5.

10. Gross, p. 3, emphasis added.

11. Gross, pp. 5, xi.

12. Gross, p. xi.

13. Gross, p. xi.

14. Gross, p. 5, emphasis added.

15. Gross, p. xi.

16. Dr. M.C. Roco, Chair, NSTC's Subcomittee on Nanoscale Science, Engineering and Technology (NSET), c/o National Science Foundation, 4201 Wilson Blvd., Suite 525, Arlington, VA 22230; E-mail: mroco@nsf.gov.

17. Zyvex Corporation Web site (<www.zyvex.com/nano/>); accessed on July 5, 2002.

18. Ralph C. Merkle, PhD, "Nanotechnology and Medicine," in *Advances in Anti-Aging Medicine,* vol. I, Dr. Ronald M. Klatz, ed. (Larchmont, NY: Mary Ann Liebert Press, Inc., 1996), pp. 277-86.

19. Merkle, in Klatz, ed., pp. 277-86.

20. Merkle, in Klatz, ed., pp. 277-86.

21. Foresight Institute Web site (<www.foresight.org>); accessed on July 5, 2002.

22. Foresight.

23. Foresight.

24. Foresight.

Chapter 15—Intelligent Design and Information Theory

1. Peter A. Angeles, *The Harper Collins Dictionary of Philosophy* (New York: HarperCollins, 1992); as cited in Tom Devartanian and Ralph O. Muncaster, *Creation vs. Evolution* videotape (Orange, CA: Petra Broadcasting Co., 2000).

2. "A Recommendation to the Association Concerning Creation," *The American Journal of Physical Anthropology,* vol. 2 (1983), pp. 457-58; as cited in Devartanian and Muncaster.

3. Richard Dawkins, *The Blind Watchmaker* (New York: W.W. Norton, 1996), p. 1, emphasis added.

4. Francis Crick, *What Mad Pursuit;* as quoted in "Science and Design," *First Things;* as cited in Devartanian and Muncaster.

5. William A. Dembski, PhD, *The Design Inference: Eliminating Chance Through Small Probabilities* (Cambridge, UK: Cambridge University Press, 1998). © Cambridge

University Press, 1998. Reprinted with the permission of Cambridge University Press (http://www.cambridge.org).

6. Dembski, *The Design Inference.*

7. Dembski, *The Design Inference.*

8. Adapted from William A. Dembski, PhD, *Intelligent Design: The Bridge Between Science and Theology* (Downers Grove, IL: InterVarsity Press, 1999), p. 134. © 1999 by William A. Dembski. Used by permission of InterVarsity Press, P.O. Box 1400, Downers Grove, IL 60515 (www.ivpress.com).

Chapter 16—Physics: How Do We Explain the Contradiction Between Two Natural Laws?

1. "Physics," *World Book Encyclopedia,* vol. 15 (Chicago: World Book, Inc., 1987), p. 440.

2. "Thermodynamics," *Microsoft® Encarta® Encyclopedia 99.* © 1993–1998 Microsoft Corporation. All rights reserved.

3. "Thermodynamics," *Encarta® Encyclopedia.*

4. Eric J. Lerner, *The Big Bang Never Happened* (New York: Random House, 1991), pp. 120, 295-318; as cited in Hugh Ross, PhD, *The Creator and the Cosmos* (Colorado Springs, CO: NavPress, 2001), p. 99. Used by permission.

5. For reference, here are the postulates of special relativity:

   • "Space and time form a 4-dimensional continuum—spacetime."

   • "There exist global spacetime frames with respect to which unaccelerated objects move in straight lines at constant velocity." [Note: this accommodates Newton's classical laws of motion from 1697.]

   • "The speed of light *c* is a universal constant, the same in any inertial frame."

   • "The laws of physics are the same in any inertial frame, regardless of position or velocity."

   (Professor Andrew J.S. Hamilton, Department of Astrophysical and Planetary Sciences, University of Colorado, Boulder [<http://casa.colorado.edu/~ajsh/home.html>, updated May 7, 2001].)

6. Albert Einstein, "Die Grundlage der allgemeinen Relativitätstheorie," *Annalen der Physik,* vol. 49 (1916), pp. 769-822. The English translation is in *The Principle of Relativity* by H.A. Lorentz, et al. (London: Methuen and Co., 1923), pp. 109-64; as cited in Ross, *The Creator and the Cosmos,* p. 23. Used by permission.

7. Albert Einstein, "Kosmologische Betrachtungen zur allgemeinen Relativitätstheorie," Sitzungsberichte der Königlich-Preussichen Akademie der Wissenschaften, Feb. 8, 1917, pp. 142-52. The English translation is in H.A. Lorentz, et al., pp. 175-88; as cited in Ross, *The Creator and the Cosmos,* p. 23. Used by permission.

8. A. Vibert Douglas, "Forty Minutes with Einstein," *Journal of the Royal Astronomical Society of Canada,* vol. 50 (1956), p. 100; as cited in Ross, *The Creator and the Cosmos,* p. 46. Used by permission.

9. For clarification, the new cosmological constant is an essential modifier to the big-bang model. The constant might be defined as a "self-stretching" property of the space–time fabric of the universe. It implies that the universe stretches itself independent of heat or light, and that as the universe expands the more stretching energy it gains. Thus, the constant is, in a sense, antigravitational. As the universe spreads out, the effect of gravity

weakens, while the effect of the cosmic stretching constant strengthens. (Ross, *The Creator and the Cosmos,* p. 45.) Used by permission.

10. *The Columbia Electronic Encyclopedia.* Copyright © 1994, 2000, Columbia University Press.

11. *The Columbia Electronic Encyclopedia.*

12. As cited in Ross, *The Creator and the Cosmos,* p. 31. Used by permission.

13. "U.S. Scientists Find a 'Holy Grail': Ripples at Edge of the Universe," London *International Herald Tribune,* April 24, 1992, p. 1; as cited in Ross, *The Creator and the Cosmos,* p. 31. Used by permission.

14. As cited in Ross, *The Creator and the Cosmos,* p. 31. Used by permission.

15. Ross, *The Creator and the Cosmos,* p. 57. Used by permission.

16. P. Jokeosen, et al., "Detection of Intergalactic Ionized Helium Absorption in a High-Redshift Quasar," *Nature,* vol. 370 (1994), pp. 35-39; and Yuri I. Izotov, et al., "Helium Abundance in the Most Metal-Deficient Blue Compact Galaxies: I Zw 18 and SBS 0335-052," *Astrophysical Journal,* vol. 527 (1999), pp. 757-77; both as cited in Ross, *The Creator and the Cosmos,* p. 57. Used by permission.

17. Ross, *The Creator and the Cosmos,* p. 60. Used by permission.

18. Hugh Ross, PhD, interview, September 7, 2001, at Reasons to Believe, Pasadena, CA.

19. Hugh Ross, *The Fingerprint of God,* 2nd ed. (Orange, CA: Promise Publishing, 1991), pp. 45-47; as cited in Hugh Ross, PhD, "Another Success for General Relativity," Reasons to Believe Web site (<www.reasons.org/resources/apologetics/success.html>).

20. Roger Penrose, *Shadows of the Mind* (New York: Oxford University Press, 1994), p. 230; as cited in Hugh Ross, *Beyond the Cosmos* (Colorado Springs, CO: NavPress, 1996), pp. 22-23; as cited in Ross, "Another Success for General Realitivity."

21. Lawrence M. Krauss, "The End of the Age Problem and the Case for a Cosmological Constant Revisited," *Astrophysical Journal,* vol. 501 (1998), p. 461; as cited in Ross, *The Creator and the Cosmos,* p. 45. Used by permission.

Chapter 17—A Finely Tuned Universe: What Are the Odds?
1. A. Vibert Douglas, "Forty Minutes with Einstein," *Journal of the Royal Astronomical Society of Canada,* vol. 50 (1956), p. 100; Lincoln Barnett, *The Universe and Dr. Einstein* (New York: William Sloane Associates, 1948), p. 106; George Smoot; all as cited in Hugh Ross, PhD, *The Creator and the Cosmos* (Colorado Springs, CO: NavPress, 2001), pp. 72,31. Used by permission.

2. Ross, p. 109. Used by permission.

3. Ross, pp. 99,113. Used by permission.

4. Lawrence M. Krauss, "The End of the Age Problem and the Case for a Cosmological Constant Revisited," *Astrophysical Journal,* vol. 501 (1998), p. 461; as cited in Ross, p. 54. Used by permission.

5. This and previous two bullet points from Ross, pp. 152-53. Used by permission.

6. Ross, pp. 195-98. Used by permission.

7. Ross, p. 198. Used by permission.

Summing Up: How to Build a Strong Bridge

1. Wernher von Braun, preface to Robert E. D. Clark, *Creation: Nature's Designs and Designer* (Mountain View, CA: Pacific Press Publishing Assoc., 1971), p. 6; as cited in John Ankerberg and John Weldon, *Darwin's Leap of Faith* (Eugene, OR: Harvest House Publishers, 1998), p. 129.

2. Robert Jastrow, *God and the Astronomers,* p. 116; as cited in <http://members.tripod.com/~Emmaus1/proofs.html>.

Appendix B—How Old Are the Earth and the Universe?
1. Dr. Robert Grange, *A Scientist Looks at Creation* videotape (Reel to Real & American Portrait Films: 1-800-736-4567).

2. Roger C. Wiens, "The Dynamics of Dating—The Reliability of Radiometric Dating Methods," *Facts for Faith* newsletter, fourth quarter, 2001, pp. 11-18.

3. Chris Stassen, "The Age of the Earth," Talk. Origins archive: last updated April 27, 1997 (<http://www.talkorigins.org/faqs/faq-age-of-the-earth.html>).

4. Stassen.

5. Craig J. Hazen, PhD, personal interview, August 29, 2001, Biola University, LaMirada, CA.

6. Information about the degree of latitude in Hebrew interpretation, along with other insights in this appendix, was obtained from Dr. William Williams, Professor of Hebrew at Vanguard University. Dr. Williams has taught Hebrew for many years and has been on the committees for five different Bible translations, including the popular New International Version.

Bibliography

Alcamo, I. Edward. *Schaum's Outline of Theory and Problems of Microbiology*. New York: McGraw Hill, 1998.

Behe, Michael J. *Darwin's Black Box: The Biochemical Challenge to Evolution*. New York: The Free Press, 1996.

Brack, André, ed. *The Molecular Origins of Life: Assembling Pieces of the Puzzle*. Cambridge, UK: Cambridge University Press, 1998.

Brouwer, Sigmund. *The Unrandom Universe*. Eugene, OR: Harvest House Publishers, 2002.

Clarke, Tom. "Raking through the embers: Clues about the origin and fate of the Universe lie hidden in the microwave radiation left over from its early days. Tom Clarke examines the latest attempts to map the Big Bang's afterglow," *Nature*, vol. 411 (June 21, 2001), www.nature.com.

Darwin, Charles. *On the Origin of the Species*, reprint of 1st ed. Cambridge, MA: Harvard University Press, 1964.

Dawkins, Richard. *The Blind Watchmaker: Why the Evidence of Evolution Reveals a Universe Without Design*. New York: W.W. Norton, 1996.

Dembski, William. *Intelligent Design: The Bridge Between Science and Theology*. Downers Grove, IL: InterVarsity Press, 1999.

————, ed. *Mere Creation: Science, Faith & Intelligent Design* (with contributions by Michael Behe, David Berlinski, Phillip Johnson, Hugh Ross, et al.). Downers Grove, IL: InterVarsity Press, 1998.

Denton, Michael. *Evolution: A Theory in Crisis, New Developments in Science Are Challenging Orthodox Darwinism.* Bethseda, MD: Adler & Adler, 1986.

Earth Science. California ed. Woodland Hills, CA: Glencoe McGraw-Hill, 2001.

Gish, Duane T. *Creation Scientists Answer Their Critics.* El Cajon, CA: Institute for Creation Research, 1993.

————. *Evolution: The Fossils Still Say No!* El Cajon, CA: Institute for Creation Research, 1995.

Goodsell, David S. *The Machinery of Life.* New York: Springer-Verlag New York, Inc., 1982.

Grange, Robert. *A Scientist Looks at Creation* (videotape). Reel to Real & American Portrait Films. For information call 1-800-736-4567.

Great Discoveries. New York: Time, Inc.

Gross, Michael. *Travels to the Nanoworld: Miniature Machinery in Nature and Technology.* Cambridge, MA: Perseus Publishing, 1999.

Hawking, Stephen W. *A Brief History of Time: From the Big Bang to Black Holes.* New York: Bantam Books, 1988.

Heeren, Fred. *Show Me God: What the Message from Space Is Telling Us About God.* Wheeling, IL: Searchlight Publications, 1995.

Herbert, David. *Charles Darwin's Religious Views: From Creationist to Evolutionist.* London, Ontario: Hersil Publishing, 1990.

Hoagland, Mahlon, and Dodson, Bert. *The Way Life Works.* New York: Random House, Inc., 1998.

Hoyle, Fred. *Mathematics of Evolution.* Memphis, TN: Acorn Enterprises, LLC, 1999.

Maynard Smith, John, and Szathmary, Eors. *The Origins of Life: From the Birth of Life to the Origins of Language.* New York: Oxford University Press, Inc., 1999.

Milton, Richard. *Shattering the Myths of Darwinism.* Rochester, VT: Park Street Press, 1997.

Moreland, J.P., ed. *The Creation Hypothesis: Scientific Evidence for an Intelligent Designer.* Downers Grove, IL: InterVarsity Press, 1994.

Morris, Henry M. *Men of Science, Men of God: Great Scientists Who Believed the Bible.* El Cajon, CA: Master Books, 1988.

————, and Gary Parker. *What Is Creation Science?* El Cajon, CA: Master Books, 1987.

Muncaster, Ralph O. *A Skeptic's Search for God.* Eugene, OR: Harvest House Publishers, 2002.

————. *Why Are Scientists Turning to God?* Eugene, OR: Harvest House Publishers, 2002.

Ridley, Matt. *Genome: The Autobiography of a Species in 23 Chapters.* New York: HarperCollins Publishers, 1999.

Ross, Hugh. *The Creator and the Cosmos.* Colorado Springs, CO: NavPress, 2001. *The Creator and the Cosmos,* Hugh Ross, © 2001. Used by permission of Nav-Press—www.navpress.com. All rights reserved.

Ruse, Michael, ed. *But Is It Science? The Philosophical Question in the Creation/ Evolution Controversy.* Amherst, NY: Prometheus Books, 1996.

Spetner, Lee. *Not By Chance: Shattering the Modern Theory of Evolution.* Brooklyn, NY: The Judaica Press, Inc., 1998.

Swenson, Richard A. *More Than Meets the Eye: Fascinating Glimpses of God's Power and Design.* Colorado Springs, CO: NavPress, 2000. *More Than Meets the Eye,* Richard Swenson, © 2000. Used by permission of NavPress—www.navpress.com. All rights reserved.

Wells, Jonathan. *Icons of Evolution: Science or Myth?: Why Much of What We Teach About Evolution Is Wrong.* Washington, D.C.: Regnery Press, 2000.

Wiens, Roger C. "The Dynamics of Dating: The Reliability of Radiometric Dating Methods." *Facts for Faith* newsletter, fourth quarter, 2001.

Wilson, Edward O. *The Diversity of Life.* New York: W.W. Norton, 1999.

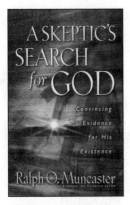

1,456 hours of Sunday school and church turned Ralph Muncaster into a hard-core atheist.

Then he was challenged to honestly investigate the Bible and the facts of modern science. He was stunned. Fact after fact—from biology, history, archaeology, physics—lined up with the Bible's account!

Join Ralph on the intensive personal search that took him—a cynical skeptic with an education in engineering—from disbelief to belief in God and the Jesus of the Bible. Along the way,

- you'll encounter the same astounding evidence that the author found during his three-year search

- you'll find solid information that challenges comfortable assumptions and outdated ideas

- your mind will be opened and your faith will be strengthened

Fascinating, unconventional, and provocative, *A Skeptic's Search for God* will point you to the facts—and to the God of the universe who is behind them.

Tough Questions—Quick, Factual, Convincing Answers

The Examine the Evidence Series
by Ralph O. Muncaster

Are There Contradictions in the Bible?

Can Archaeology Prove the New Testament?

Can Archaeology Prove the Old Testament?

Can We Know for Certain We Are Going to Heaven?

Can You Trust the Bible?

Creation vs. Evolution:
What Do the Latest Scientific Discoveries Reveal?

Creation vs. Evolution VIDEO:
What Do the Latest Scientific Discoveries Reveal?

Does Prayer Really Work?

Does the Bible Predict the Future?

How Do We Know Jesus Was God?

How Is Jesus Different from Other Religious Leaders?

How to Talk About Jesus with the Skeptics in Your Life

Is the Bible Really a Message from God?

Science—Was the Bible Ahead of Its Time?

What Is the Proof for the Resurrection?

What Is the Trinity?

What Really Happens When You Die?

Why Are Scientists Turning to God?

Why Does God Allow Suffering?